Answering the Call

W elcome to this glimpse into the fascinating world of emergency aviation, where fixed-wing and rotary aircraft are transformed into police cars, ambulances, firefighters, search vehicles, humanitarian rescuers, border patrollers and infrastructure workstations.

It's a world in which many of us will never participate, but if we do need help in an emergency the sight of a hovering helicopter, landing airplane or approaching drone will offer relief and reassurance. Every day, aircraft are saving lives and averting disasters, a service that started when a group of German doctors decided to do something about people dying on the roads due to medical care not arriving in time.

Emergency services can be as broad as the imagination, but this volume focuses on aircraft operating missions in firefighting, emergency medical services, law enforcement, search and rescue, border protection and infrastructure recovery after disasters. Specialists from major operators such as the Royal Flying Doctor Service, Coulson Aviation, CAL FIRE, McDermott Aviation and the UK's National Police Air Service have shared their experiences to give you insight into what they do and how they do it. We look at the aircraft and equipment they use and the challenges they are overcoming as climates change and wildfires, floods and other natural disasters become more common.

The aircraft operating these missions are an eclectic mix of old and new, including Air Cranes, Chinooks, Black Hawks, C-130 Hercules, Kaman K-MAXs and even unmanned air vehicles. Fixed-wing aircraft such the ever reliable King Air, Challenger, Pilatus PC-12 and Cessnas dominate, although one you may not have heard of is the Italian Vulcanair P68R used for law enforcement missions.

The section on unmanned aircraft gives a peek into this emerging sector of aviation. It is not just about delivering cups of coffee or a bag of screws via small commercial drones, but rather shows how an uncrewed Black Hawk can be piloted by an operator on the ground with a handheld tablet to extinguish wildfires.

It has been a privilege to talk with the men and women who run towards danger to protect the rest of us or to provide care when we are in desperate situations. I hope you enjoy this look into their world.

Michael Doran
Editor

▼ Air ambulances are lifesavers in serious vehicle accidents. Airbus

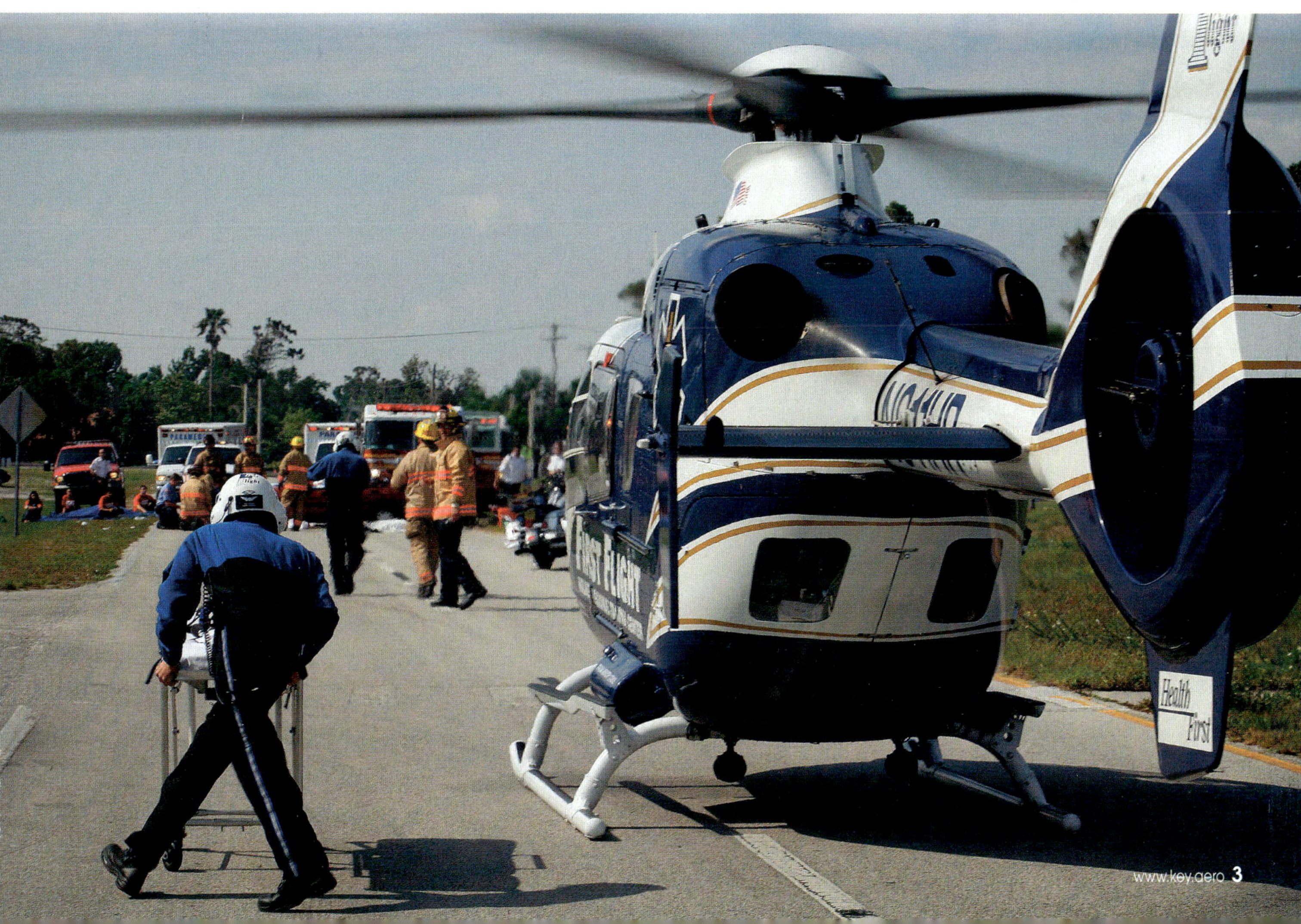

Contents

Coulson Aviation

ISBN: 978 1 83632 115 6
Editor: Michael Doran
Senior editor, specials: Roger Mortimer
Email: roger.mortimer@keypublishing.com
Cover Design: Steve Donovan
Design: SJmagic DESIGN SERVICES, India
Advertising Sales Manager: Sam Clark
Email: sam.clark@keypublishing.com
Tel: 01780 755131
Advertising Production: Becky Antoniades
Email: Rebecca.antoniades@keypublishing.com

SUBSCRIPTION/MAIL ORDER
Key Publishing Ltd, PO Box 300, Stamford, Lincs, PE9 1NA
Tel: 01780 480404
Subscriptions email: subs@keypublishing.com
Mail Order email: orders@keypublishing.com

Website: www.keypublishing.com/shop

PUBLISHING
Group CEO: Adrian Cox
Publisher: Steve O'Hara
Published by:
Key Publishing Ltd, PO Box 100, Stamford, Lincs, PE9 1XQ
Tel: 01780 755131 Website: www.keypublishing.com

PRINTING
Precision Colour Printing Ltd, Haldane, Halesfield 1, Telford, Shropshire. TF7 4QQ

DISTRIBUTION
Seymour Distribution Ltd, 2 Poultry Avenue, London, EC1A 9PU
Enquiries Line: 02074 294000.

Sky Guardians

Aircraft of almost all shapes, sizes and age are engaged in keeping communities safe and offering aid when it's needed most.

▶ **Humanitarian aid delivered by Samaritan's Purse.** Samaritan's Purse

*S*OS AIR Special Services Aviation is a comprehensive review of how aircraft have fundamentally changed the face of firefighting, law enforcement, emergency medicine, search and rescue, border protection and infrastructure security. This publication is not only about the aircraft but also takes readers behind the scenes to hear from operators about their missions and the challenges they face.

That includes an inside look into the early 2025 wildfires in southern California through the eyes of CAL FIRE, the firefighting agency that was battling to save the citizens and properties of Los Angeles. It explains how the team at CAL FIRE managed go above and beyond and take the performance of their fixed wing and rotary aircraft to the limit.

In some sectors of the emergency services, such as aerial firefighting, those challenges are going through a paradigm shift as climates change and threats become a year-round event, not just something that happens in the hot, dry summer months. That change has produced a shortage of large airtankers, with governments and fire agencies now scrambling to secure these aircraft when there are not enough to meet demand.

Aerial firefighting specialists McDermott Aviation in Australia and Canada's Coulson Aviation

▼ **Large airtankers are often the only defence against wildfires.** Erickson

understand that the industry needs more resources at their disposal. To help fill that gap, Coulson is scouring the world for Lockheed Martin C-130 Hercules aircraft to repurpose as tankers and McDermott, whose pedigree is operating helicopters, is going a step further by setting up a manufacturing facility to put the Bell 214ST back into production.

Four other organisations recognised this growing imbalance between supply and demand as an opportunity and unveiled their plans for new turboprop airtankers. One is a totally clean-sheet design from an Italian company and the other three are taking existing turboprop platforms and modifying them extensively.

Aeromedical services operate a mix of air ambulance and emergency medical aircraft that have changed the way patient recovery is handled, saving thousands of lives. Air ambulance missions are typically repatriations or transfers using fixed-wing aircraft such as Challenger 605, Pilatus PC-24 and Cessna Citation jets, while emergency services tend to rely on helicopters. This is a field where the aircraft configuration and specialised medical equipment make all the difference, so operators have a wide array of aircraft platforms to choose from. The choice depends on the operating environments and economics, but popular types include the Airbus H135 and H145, Leonardo AW 139 and AW169 helicopters and Beechcraft King Air and Pilatus PC-12 turboprops.

Search and rescue can be operated by parapublic agencies, military forces or a combination of both. Again, it is the mission equipment that sets this field apart from general aviation, with longer range fixed-wing aircraft favoured for maritime searches, such as the operation mounted for the missing Malaysia Airlines Boeing 777.

It is no easy feat to hover a large helicopter just metres from a cliff face or above a vessel at night in low visibility or severe weather conditions. Advances in autopilot technology and other aircraft stability controls have aided the process, but ultimately it is the pilot, assisted by his crew hanging out the aircraft, who make it happen.

Helicopters can perform rescue missions at sea when the conditions don't allow a vessel to operate and can deploy a crewman to an injured person where ground crews are unable to access the location or will take too long to deliver aid. Tracking technology has made finding people bobbing about in a lifeboat or sheltering in a forest possible, but it is the helicopter and its crew that get people the help they need.

Perhaps the most well-known use of helicopters operating special services is in law enforcement and border protection, with a plethora of TV shows showcasing their daily work. Aircraft used by multiple forces include the Leonardo AW139, Airbus H135, Bell 425 and 505 helicopters and Cessna Grand Caravans and King Air 350 aircraft. The surveillance systems allow police to find vehicles that are not yet in view and to pinpoint the exact position of anything thrown out of a vehicle being pursued, such as narcotics, weapons or clothing. The images are so clear that they are used to build irrefutable prosecution cases when offenders are brought to trial.

Aircraft also operate special missions in customs and border protection, anti-terrorism, infrastructure protection and restoration, and large scale evacuations in natural disasters. This publication is a tribute to the crews and the aircraft that work 24/7 in all conditions to keep us safe and secure.

▲ Search and rescue services fly in all weather conditions. Airbus

▲◄ Emergency medical services save lives every day. Sikorsky

◄ Law enforcement aircraft carry HD imaging. Bell

The dictionary defines an all-rounder as "a person of great versatility or wide-ranging skills", which could easily be a description of Australia's largest privately owned helicopter operator, McDermott Aviation (MA). From humble beginnings in Queensland, the company has grown to operate more than 50 aircraft from bases around Australia and in Papua New Guinea, New Caledonia and Greece.

The business was founded by CEO John McDermott in 1982 and since then has developed specialties in aerial firefighting, emergency response, heavy lifting, agricultural spraying, infrastructure support, tourism and training. It also has major maintenance facilities in the US and, in March 2025, acquired Canadian company Transwest Helicopters.

MA's helicopter fleet includes 14 Bell 214STs, 16 Bell 214Bs, four Bell 206 LongRangers, four Bell 47Ts, seven Airbus AS355 Twin Squirrels and six AS365 Dauphins. The company owns the type certificates for both the Bell 214B and 214ST series and is currently preparing to commence production of the 214ST, which John McDermott said would be known as the McDermott B214ST.

Not content with manufacturing helicopters, McDermott also revealed that the company has purchased six Transall C-160 military transport aircraft from the Luftwaffe (German Air Force). The Transall C-160 is a twin-engined version of the C-130 Hercules and will be modified to operate as a large airtanker.

▼ **McDermott Aviation operates firefighting missions internationally.**
McDermott Aviation

Aussie All-rounder

When Australia's leading helicopter operator had trouble getting technical support for its fleet of Bell 214s, the CEO decided to buy the type certificates and start building them.

▲ CEO John McDermott is a big fan of the Bell 214ST.
McDermott Aviation

▲▶ Air transport is the only way to ensure timely transfers.
McDermott Aviation

Changing markets

MA started life operating agricultural services such as crop dusting, which led to its involvement in aerial firefighting. Currently, it operates 35 rotary aircraft dedicated to firefighting and has been performing these services in Greece for five years. It also has contracts in other parts of the world and, with wildfires no longer confined to just the summer months, moves assets around the world as required.

With shipping times unreliable, the only way to move aircraft in a timely way is by air, which is a very expensive exercise. McDermott said the problem fire agencies have at the moment is that they are inconsistent with their accuracy of service periods: "For instance, fire seasons are no longer starting on August 1, then finishing on November 30. They start earlier or later and go longer, so it's really difficult, to the point of being impossible, to forecast."

Aerial firefighting contracts are typically long-term agreements that run for five or ten years, which seemingly give certainty to operators and the agencies. McDermott pointed out that the length of the contract is not the key issue, because income depends on how many days the contract covers: "We're paying £96,000 per airframe for insurance per year and if you can only amortise that across an 84-day contract it's making the price to the end user very expensive. But if the contract is for 140 days they are getting a longer service period and the cost is the same."

Firefighting operations

In May 2025, MA despatched six B214STs that were being airlifted to Greece to support firefighting efforts for the summer season, which officially runs from May 1 to October 31. These will reinforce the six already stationed in Greece and an additional three en route from the company's US operations.

In 2024, McDermott deployed 14 helicopters to Greece that operated more than 4,000 hours across 120 days and dropped more than 25,000 loads, which is approximately 75 million litres of water. According to John: "We've got a pretty sizeable facility in Elefsina and we are there year-round, because we are also doing their high mountain rescue work. That's the beauty of the 214,

▶ John McDermott is leading the charge into manufacturing.
McDermott Aviation

▼ Bell 214STs are ideal for firefighting missions.
McDermott Aviation

because we can put a winch on the side and a crewman on board and go and winch somebody off a mountain or out of the ocean."

Around 80% of MA's work in Greece is done on dry islands that have no water sources, so for aircraft to be fully effective they have to scoop water from the sea for a quick return to the fire. To solve that issue, John said the team designed and built a water scooping system to capture salt water without ingesting it into engines or airframes: "We've always been ahead of the game with design and most of our equipment on a helicopter we either designed ourselves or had a big input into it. That made us become a bit innovative – the system we designed allows us to fly along at about 25kts and scoop and pump water into the tanks.

"It's called a positive flow fill system, so it allows us to fly reasonably slow by comparison and force the water up into our existing hover pump and then the pump does the rest. It pumps the water up, so we don't have to fly as fast to force the water through the tubes."

Grecian ways

Operating in Greece requires a local fireman to be on board, which John said is mainly to avoid any language barriers. That requirement means that an operator has to use transport category aircraft, which is another reason the Bell 412 is an ideal fit for operations.

Wildfires behave and burn differently in various regions, with North American fires fought from the fuel on the ground up, while Australian fires are generally spread across the forest canopy, taking advantage of the abundant fuel in native trees. These differences mean that the tactics used also differ,

which John pointed out is the case in Greece: "I'd say the Greeks are far more proactive and are very much more concentrated on initial attack. So last year we flew a lot of hours, but we responded to nearly twice as many fires as the year before, but they burned half as much country. So they are very proactive and

▲ Bell 214STs being loaded for the long flight to Greece.
McDermott Aviation

◀ McDermott Aviation has a fleet of more than 50 helicopters.
McDermott Aviation

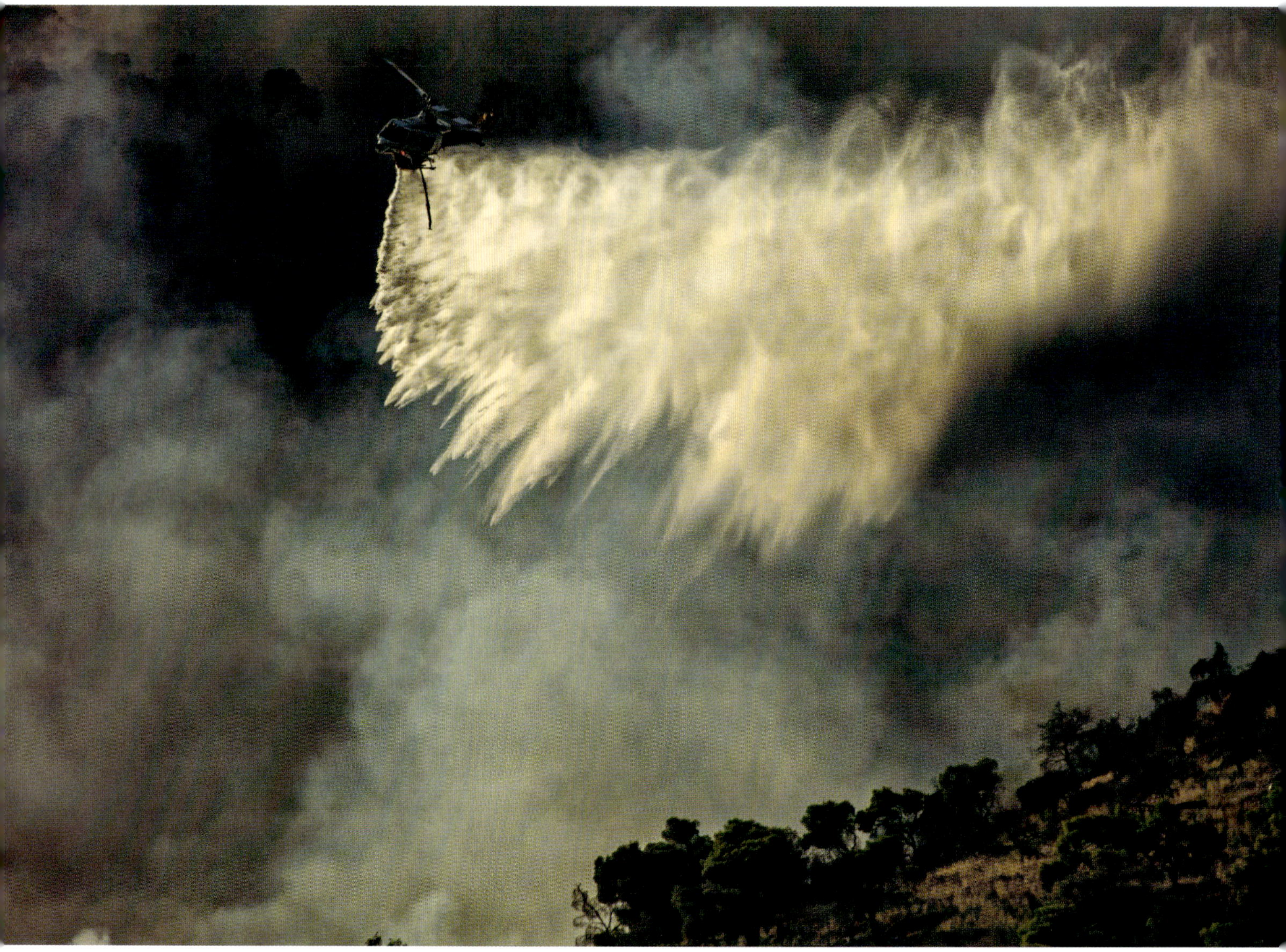

▲ **McDermott pilots are trained for precision drops.** McDermott Aviation

much more focused on initial attack in Greece."

It's an approach John prefers as it gets fires extinguished more quickly than the models in some other countries, which allow fires to burn or trickle along during the day, but as the wind picks up they need to call in the aerial assets, which in some cases can be too late to be effective.

MA has around 50 staff stationed in Greece on a rotational basis and in the fire season there are approximately 200 people directly involved in MA's operations there, including local Greek co-ordinators, liaison officers and company personnel. In 2024, MA was involved in battling raging fires that tore through Athens, forcing thousands to evacuate the city, as well as firefighting near Marathonas Lake and Penteli Mountain.

The B214 STs proved their versatility in 2023, when they were urgently deployed after torrential rain caused widespread flooding and mudslides, prompting a critical mission to rescue those trapped. John said: "We were fighting fires one night and then that night there was a massive downpour of rain. So we ended up doing evacuation work and the next day five of our helicopters rescued 192 people from the floods."

That situation is a good example of the versatility of the 214s to operate multiple roles, switching from firefighting one night and rescuing flood victims the next, which is possible because they are transport-certified and can carry passengers and cargo: "In Queensland in 2025, we did about 60 hours of aerial firefighting across our fleet, but we also did more than 250 hours of flood relief work, which is why it's important to have an aircraft that's versatile. If you're in a Black Hawk or Skycrane, you're just an aerial firefighter by design and limitations."

214ST Revival

The Bell 214ST is the largest of the Bell Huey family and was designed to meet the requirements of the Imperial Iranian Air Force but, following the Islamic Revolution of 1979, it was never delivered to Iran. It was Bell's largest conventional

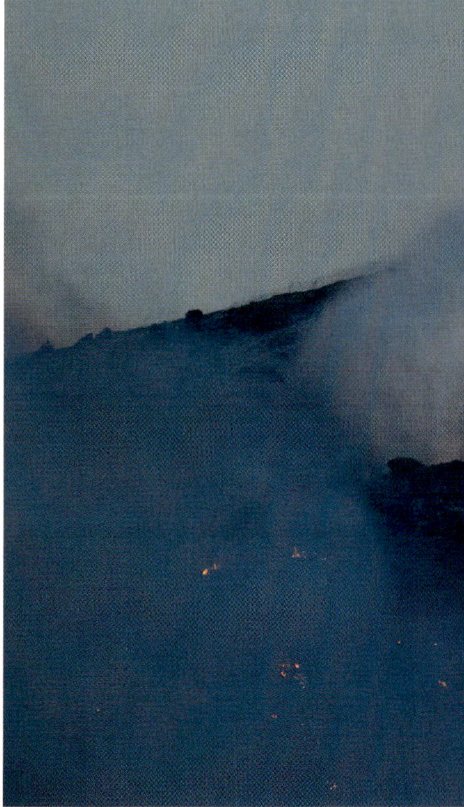

▶ **Aerial firefighting continues in all weathers and low visibility.** McDermott Aviation

helicopter until the development of the Bell 525 that first flew in 2015.

Less than 100 214STs were built between 1979-1993, when the aircraft went out of production. MA has been operating the aircraft since 2012 and the Bell 214B since 2004. Bell sold the type certificates (TCs) for the 214ST and 214B to Erickson in 2020 and McDermott later brought them from Erickson. The impetus behind acquiring the TCs was that neither Bell nor Erickson could provide MA with the support it needed and, with demand for aircraft rising, McDermott took control of the situation by buying them: "We've created a massive market for our aircraft and company and we started getting asked for more and more helicopters, but they just don't exist because we've got them all. We were asked to quote to supply around 25 for a fire agency, but they had to be new-build or built after 2020, so we basically said 'Let's build them'."

Firefighting puts significantly more strain on aircraft than almost any other field of aviation, which is why operators who specialise in it prefer to use legacy airframes, such as the S-64 Air Crane, Black Hawk, Chinook, Bell 214ST and C-130 Hercules: "The Black Hawk is becoming a major player in firefighting because they are very well built. Then you go to the Chinook, which are also well built and made from metal, not from plastic, and the Skycrane is made from cast-iron. Agencies want new aircraft, but they are just not resilient

◀ In 2024, McDermott 214s flew more than 4,000 hours in Greece. McDermott Aviation

▼ Quick refilling is vital for effective firefighting. McDermott Aviation

or strong enough to do what's involved in aerial firefighting.

"That's where we find ourselves now. We are actually building all the engine parts for the T5508D which is on our 214B, which we've been doing for about ten years. And now we're building all the parts for the 214B and 214ST. That includes the modernisation of the cockpit and improvements in various parts of the airframe."

MA engineers have reduced the weight to 4.1 metric tonnes and other changes have added a new Genesys-developed avionics suite and lowered the not-to-exceed speed to 120kt. The skidded landing gear has been heightened to allow for a tank with a capacity of 845 US gallons and the aircraft can be operated with an underslung bucket.

It is hard to imagine many operators who would value an aircraft enough to jump in headfirst and start manufacturing something that has been out of production for more than 45 years. It is even more surprising to be doing it when aviation is dealing with a massive skills shortage and ongoing supply chain disruptions.

Assembling the supply chain is well underway. To get started, MA went back to one of the US manufacturers that was involved in building the 214 programme helicopters. As luck would have it, that business had just completed a contract with Bell to build military helicopters and had the capacity to take on the project. John said: "When we bought the type certificates, we got all the tooling off Bell to build 90% of the

aircraft and now a lot of people who were involved in the 214 programme are coming out of the woodwork to help. We're in the final stages of costing it all out and what happens is now we're gearing up to build our initial run of 25 helicopters. I think we basically got most of them sold or spoken for. We hope the run will be 50 and it will be done at a rate of 12 to 15 a year once the first McDermott B214ST comes off the assembly line."

While no confirmed date has been set for an entry into service, John said the first 214ST will come off the assembly line 18 months after work started. He that added a start-up date is "probably a couple of months away", but said that the 214ST is already certified, so there will be none of the lengthy regulatory delays associated with new-builds.

Transall C-160

Running an international helicopter operation and launching the production of Bell 214STs in the US would seem be enough for any executive to look after. Not content with that, John is also eagerly awaiting regulatory clearance to launch the modified Transall C-160 large airtanker.

There is a global shortage of large airtankers, although Canada's Coulson Aviation is working to bring more C-130 Hercules to the market. With a wingspan of 40m, the Transall C-160 is a significant step up in size for MA, but John is confident about the opportunities the six aircraft will produce: "We bought them from the Luftwaffe with all their spares, which I think included 28 spare engines, 40 or 50 propeller assemblies, 30 or 40 APUs and more. The Luftwaffe had a fleet of nearly 40 C-160s and we got the last six that were flying before they were retired and dismantled."

The Transall was developed in the 1960s by the Franco-German consortium Transporter Allianz. The twin-engined jet transport aircraft flew with the air forces of Germany, France and Turkey, asw ell as some civilian operators, including the Red Cross, which operated it for

humanitarian missions delivering food and aid. It was mainly used for transporting personnel and materiel, dropping paratroopers and loads, as well as transporting injured people with medical assistance from a danger zone. The Luftwaffe received 110 of the 214 built and, from 2013, the Transall was gradually replaced by France, Germany and Turkey with the Airbus A400M.

John said the C-160 is more versatile than C-130 Hercules due to its low tyre pressure of 55 psi, which means the aircraft can operate in and out of just about any unprepared airstrip. The internal tank will have a capacity of up to 14,000 litres and the first modified aircraft is completed and awaiting clearance by CASA, Australia's aviation regulator.

Other missions

Machjet International (MI) is a sister company of MA that evolved in 2006 to support MA's aerial firefighting fleet across Australia and New Caledonia. This allowed MA to transport its crews, parts and equipment on a schedule that suited its operations, rather than rely on commercial operators.

Since then, MI has become one of Australia's leading fixed-wing charter companies, with a fleet that includes Bombardier Challengers, Cessna Citations and Beechcraft King Airs. It is also the specialist medevac operator in the MA group, offering services such as air ambulance and organ transfers with critical care paramedics on board.

MI operates fixed based operations 24/7 from two locations in Queensland and can support

any type of aeromedical operation, from basic patient transport through to high acuity medical retrieval. The Bombardier Challenger 605 and the Cessna Citation jet fleet can be reconfigured into a full air ambulance service as needed.

The jets are fitted with advanced Spectrum Aeromed powered lay-flat stretcher systems and can be fitted with a Spectrum Intensive Care Unit with full oxygen. For remote, non-sealed runway access, the King Air fleet can also be stretcher configured, offering additional versatility and accessibility.

MA's fleet can conduct search and rescue operations and often performs missions for the Australian Maritime Safety Agency. Some of the airframes are fitted with accurate directional finders or homing systems that allow for the quick and accurate location of emergency locator beacons, such as those found in boats, liferafts or aircraft.

Many MA aircraft are fitted with personnel winches and can also be equipped with rescue strops, rescue baskets, deployable survival kits, liferings, sea dyes and other safety and rescue gear. As a minimum, crews are trained in first aid, while rescue swimmers qualified for helicopter extraction are available when needed.

▼◄ **Protecting life and assets is the aim of aerial firefighting.**
McDermott Aviation

▼ **Finding water can be tricky in dry summer locations.**
McDermott Aviation

Aerial Firefighting

Leaving aside the politics of climate change, there is no question that drier winters and longer summers are changing the nature of wildfires and, in turn, shifting the paradigm of how aerial firefighting is structured.

The devastating fires in California, Europe and South Korea in early 2025 upended the notion that wildfires were only a seasonal occurrence and that the aerial assets and crews could be contracted and shifted around the world on a regular schedule. Simply put, governments and fire agencies want the assets, such as large air tankers like the Chinook CH-47, Erickson Air Crane and Hercules C-130, to arrive earlier and stay longer and there are not enough of those aircraft to allow that to happen.

The high cost of acquiring and operating these assets is out of reach for some nations who have previously relied on the steady seasonal movement pattern that is now questionable. Unpredictable fire seasons appear to be here to stay, but when they hit, such as in Los Angeles, the cost is enormous, not to mention the massive emissions hit to the environment.

An interesting aspect of aerial firefighting is that many of the aircraft used have been flying for decades and it's not uncommon to see airframes operating well beyond their expected retirement. The reality is that Black Hawks, Chinooks, Air Cranes and Hercules C-130s are made for tough work in extreme environments and give the high reliability that's vital in this sector.

CAL FIRE

The California Department of Forestry and Fire Protection, otherwise known as CAL FIRE, is dedicated to the fire prevention and protection and stewardship of more than 31m acres of California's privately owned wildlands. It also provides varied emergency services in 36 of the state's 50 counties via contracts with local governments.

It is first in line when major disasters striker the state, such as the devastating wildfires in Southern California and the Los Angeles area in early 2025. CAL FIRE battled those blazes with non-stop day and night operations that pushed the organisation to its limits in what was typically the offseason for Californian forest fires.

CAL FIRE operates the world's largest civil aerial firefighting fleet, with rotary and fixed-wing aircraft situated at 14 air tanker bases around the state, ten CAL FIRE helitack bases and one CAL FIRE/ San Diego County Sheriff helitack airfield. This dispersed network

▼ At CAL FIRE, Grumman S-2T Tankers are the fleet workhorses. CAL FIRE

means that aircraft can reach even the most remote regions within the State Responsibility Area in as little as 20 minutes.

CAL FIRE's fleet of air tankers, tactical aircraft and helicopters are managed under the Aviation Management Program headquartered at McClellan Airfield near Sacramento. It has a fleet of more than 60 fixed and rotary wing aircraft, including a second C-130 Hercules tanker that was acquired in April 2025. The fleet comprises Grumman S-2T and C-130 Hercules tankers, Sikorsky S-70i FIRE HAWK and Bell UH-1H Super Huey helicopters and North American OV-10A Bronco Air Tactical aircraft. The first CAL FIRE C-130 arrived in 2024 and five more of the former US Coast Guard aircraft will follow as per legislation signed by US President Joe Biden in 2023.

Following their arrival at CAL FIRE, the C-130s were extensively modified, including the installation of a 4000-gallon tank and a sophisticated retardant delivery system. Before handing them over the USAF and the US Coast Guard undertook maintenance support that included replacing the inner and outer wing boxes and essential spare parts.

California is the first US state to own and operate a C-130 for fighting wildfires and CAL FIRE has also installed a C-130 simulator which is the only one of its kind in the US to be owned by a fire department. The first C-130 played a critical role in the Los Angeles fires in early 2025, and

with a second now in the service CAL FIRE has significantly more firepower at its disposal.

A feature of CAL FIRE's operations are its ten helitack bases, from which aircraft not only head to fires but also deliver attack teams and resources to support ground crews. Much of modern firefighting strategy is based around detecting a fire early and applying maximum resources and aerial support as quickly as possible to contain it before it spreads.

CAL FIRE's aviation communications officer Linnea Edmeier described helitack teams

as akin to a fire engine leaving the station with its crew on board the tanker, who then start fighting a fire as soon as they arrive at the scene: "The goal of all our aviation assets is to support the ground crews, so we're on a helicopter, go to the fire, deploy onto the fire and then the helicopter supports us with drops. We have a specially trained fire captain who is the front seat captain and assists the pilot by working the radios, communicating with the pilot and providing assistance."

The service is working through a transition from the Bell Super Huey to the S-70 FIREHAWK as the primary fire

▲ FIRE HAWKs have an internal tank carrying 1,000g of water. CAL FIRE

▼ A CAL FIRE S-70i FIRE HAWK tackling the 2025 Los Angeles fires. CAL FIRE

▲ CAL FIRE's C-130s were formerly operated by the US Coast Guard. CAL FIRE

line helicopter. The Hueys will still be operated for fuel reduction projects and other missions, but the larger FIRE HAWK can accommodate more crew members and drop 1,000g of water, nearly three times more than the 360g carried by the Huey.

CAL FIRE was an early adopter of aerial night firefighting and has been operating those missions for more than four years. Attacking fires in the dark, when temperatures and winds tend to drop and humidity rise, makes aerial firefighting significantly more effective and the FIRE HAWKs are compatible with night-vision goggles (NVGs) and systems.

To add more resources, CAL FIRE contracts other fixed-wing and rotary operators during the summer on an exclusive-use basis and increasingly brings in operators that are NVG-capable. It is also steadily increasing the number of its bases that can fly night ops, which were a key part of its strategy in the 2025 Los Angeles fires.

To increase its effectiveness, in 2024 CAL FIRE assembled its exclusive-use operators along with its helicopter co-ordinators and NVG-capable base crews for a training exercise. This ran for two weeks, with multiple helicopters in the air at night, building capability that was used in later fires that proved the system's effectiveness.

Edmeier said: "When the Palisades fires came around, we were ready to launch, with aircraft rotating in and out every few hours from a 24-hour-staffed helibase with upwards of 50 helicopters. Typically, we may shut down around three or four o'clock in the morning with a skeleton crew at the base, but this was a 24-hour helibase and all the 'copters stayed in there and held the fire as it was coming into a neighbourhood."

CAL FIRE fields 16 North American OV-10 Air Tactical Aircraft, some of which were originally used by US Marines between 1968 and 1993 as counter insurgency aircraft and close air support to military forces. These are used as control and command platforms for aerial firefighting from which the air attack officer (AAO) co-ordinates with the incident commander on the ground. The AAO is a highly trained and experienced fire officer who calls in aircraft and works with ground crews to set priorities, identify potential threats to life and property, and establish where to make retardant and water drops. The OV-10 Broncos can also be used as lead planes for very large air tankers when not working as a command and control platform.

Down under

In Australia, the ubiquitous orange Air Cranes usually arrive in November to stay for the summer, then pack up in March and head to European hotspots such as Greece and Spain, before transiting to the US for a tour of duty there. Time has to be found

▼ A CAL FIRE pilot feels the heat in the 2025 LA wildfires. CAL FIRE

for annual maintenance, crew training and time off, before the circus winds up again to head back down under.

Australia's National Aerial Firefighting Centre operates a national scheme that provides aircraft to various state and territory agencies. In 2024/2025 it contracted 150 aircraft nationally, with approximately another 300 aircraft available as and when needed. The contracted fleet includes multiple types, such as the Hercules C-130, Air Tractor AT-802, Cessna 208 and Bombardier Dash 8-400 aircraft, along with Black Hawk, Air Crane, Bell 214 and Airbus Super Puma helicopters.

In New South Wales, the Rural Fire Service (RFS) has taken the process in-house by owning its own fleet, which became a priority after the disastrous Black Summer bushfires in 2020. The RFS fleet comprises an impressive line-up of 11 aircraft, including a 737 FIRELINER, Chinook CH-47, two Cessna Citations, one Beechcraft Super King Air and six Bell 214 helicopters. The fleet is also used to support other services, such as the NSW State Emergency Service for rescues during floods.

In July 2024, the RFS awarded Coulson Aviation Australia a ten-year contract to oversee the management, operation and maintenance of the aircraft. Coulson had managed the majority of the RFS fleet for the previous five years and has been a strong supporter of firefighting in Australia for the last decade.

▲ The agency is transitioning from the Huey to the FIRE HAWK. CAL FIRE

◄ Air Cranes can quickly refill and return for another drop. Kestrel

▼ There are two C-130s in the fleet, with five more to follow. CAL FIRE

To facilitate night-time firefighting, the CH-47 Chinook has been fitted with a larger internal tank and can now deliver 2,900 US gal of water, which makes it the largest capacity helicopter in Australia and second only to the RFS 737 tanker. It had previously operated with a 10,000-litre bucket, but that was too dangerous to use at night or over densely populated areas.

The New South Wales government and the RFS have taken a bold move to assemble their own fleet of large and expensive tankers, but no doubt there will be many other agencies around the world now assessing their particular needs. However finding and converting these legacy aircraft is not always a quick or simple process, which is why some new start-ups with revolutionary idea for tankers are on the horizon.

Comparing Chinooks

US company Columbia Helicopters is the global leader in heavy-lift rotorcraft operations and the OEM for the 234 Chinook and Vertol 107-II. It is also the FAA type certificate holder for the CH-47D, an ex-military helicopter that transfers into the civilian fleet as a restricted category aircraft.

The 234 Chinook is based on the CH-47 Chinook and the Vertol 107-II on the CH-46 Sea Knight. The 234 has a maximum gross weight of 51,000lb, a range of 560nm and can operate

with an external bucket or an internal dual tank system that includes a 140 US gal retardant reservoir and a 2,800 US gal water tank.

The smaller 107-II operates with a bucket suspended under the aircraft that can drop 1,300 US gal and can be filled in 90 seconds from water sources as shallow as 18in. The 107-II can carry up to 26 passengers and operate missions such as firefighting, humanitarian aid, heavy lift, oil and gas and infrastructure operations.

In March 2025, Columbia Helicopters renewed its aerial firefighting contract with CMC Savunma Sanayi (CMC) in Turkey. This is its fifth consecutive season supporting Turkey's national wildfire response and reinforces Columbia's strong partnership with CMC and the Turkish General Directorate of Forestry. For the 2025 fire season, Columbia will deploy four 234 Multi-Misson Chinooks and a support team of experienced flight crews and maintenance personnel. Each aircraft is equipped with a 2,600 US gal Bambi Bucket. They will have their work cut out for them as data from the General Directorate of Forestry indicates an increase in annual wildfire incidents from approximately 2,950 in 2020 to an estimated 3,800 in 2024.

Avincis helps out

From its headquarters in Lisbon, Avincis is one of world's leading

▼ Columbia Helicopters' 234 Chinooks have a 2,800g tank.
Columbia Helicopters

pilots, crews, technicians and support teams. The rotary fleet includes Airbus EC145C2, H145D2, H145D3 and Super Puma L2, Bell 412, Sikorsky S76 and Leonardo AW109, AW139 and AW169 helicopters, while the fixed wing aeroplanes include Beechcraft, Cessna and Canadair CL-215 and CL-415 types.

In May 2025 Avincis mobilised two of its Canadair CL-415 firebombers from its Italian base to join crews already fighting a significant wildfire in Israel. Within 24 hours of receiving the request from the Israeli government, the two aircraft had left Rome and were on their way to Tel Aviv.

The CL-415s can release more than 1,600 US gal of water with every drop. In 2024, they provided additional support at large wildfires in Greece, Albania and Portugal. There are 18 of the type in the Avincis fleet based around Italy, including at stations in Rome, Lamezia, Genoa, Olbia, Trapani and Naples.

Predictive modelling

New Zealand technology business TracPlus is the leading provider of mission-critical intelligence for firefighting operations and, in April 2025, it announced the launch of its next-generation FireFlyte platform. The secure cloud-based platform is designed to provide real-time

▲ **In Australia it is common for helicopters to refill from private dams.** Columbia Helicopters

▼ **Columbia 234 Chinooks are based on the military CH-47.** Columbia Helicopters

emergency aerial services operators, with a focus on aerial firefighting, emergency medical services, air ambulance services, search and rescue and aerial transport for oil and gas platforms. The company is the largest provider of emergency aerial services in Europe, with additional operations in Africa and South America, although it often operates invisibly on behalf

of customers who are primarily government organisations.

Avincis operates from more than 180 bases across Spain, Portugal, Italy, Norway, Sweden, Finland, Mozambique and Chile. It has a fleet of approximately 220 aircraft, including 180 helicopters and 40 fixed wing airframes and operates its aircraft with a team of more than 2,400 people, including experienced

intelligence for more efficient, safer and effective aerial firefighting operations.

FireFlyte enhances inter-agency collaboration, allowing multiple teams and organisations to share critical insights, co-ordinate response efforts and improve overall firefighting effectiveness. Chief marketing and sales officer Todd O'Hara said the best way to look at the system is in two parts, operator and agency use: "The operators primarily use the product as a safety tool that tracks their aircraft through satellites and cellular networks. The agencies are the ones paying for the work, so they use the data to see where all their assets are and as a despatch tool."

The location data tells the system when the aircraft have started moving and are climbing to start breaking up the different phases of flight into blocks, such as taxiing, take-off, landing, etc. That gives all sections of the business the information they need for their roles and establish what the operator can charge the agency for the service. When an incident happens, the agencies need to know the location of individual aircraft, so they can send the closest asset, although in some jurisdictions

▲ In 2025, Avincis sent two Canadair CL-145 firebombers to fight Israeli fires. Avincis

▼ The TracPlus FireFlyte system helps operators manage their fleets and costs. TracPlus

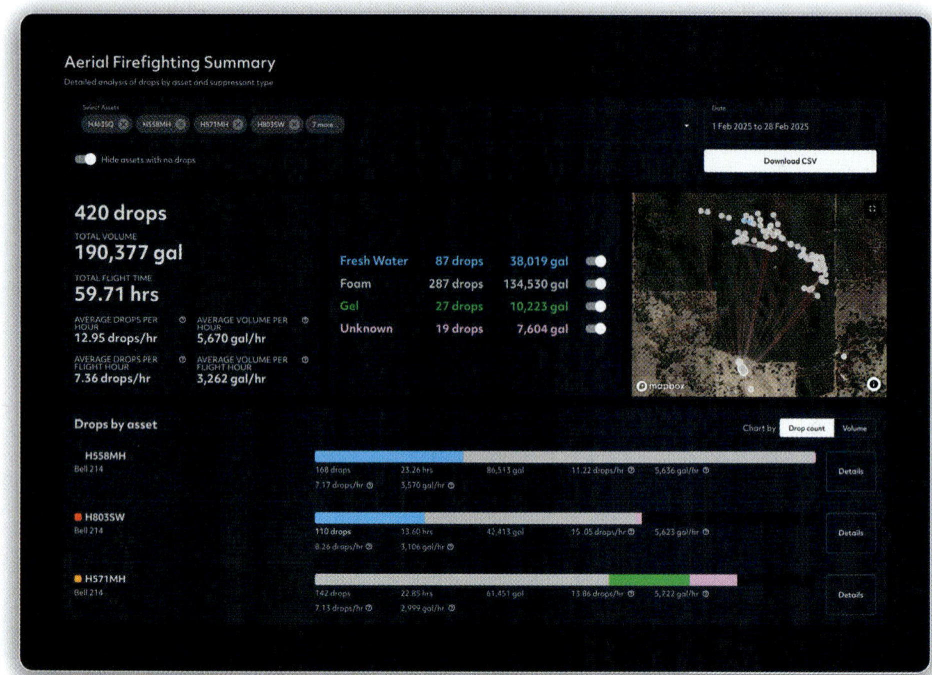

▲ **FireFlyte allows operators to track their firefighting operations.** TracPlus

FireFlyte presents a picture of the predicted size of the fire, how it will behave and what assets will be needed. O'Hara explained: "(In that case) we should pre-position assets to those locations, otherwise the response time will be 30 minutes from where they are located now. By moving them closer, we can get a ten minute response time. We're using the data to inform things ahead of time, rather than real-time."

The system also allows agencies and operators to look back on previous fires in any area and see what it took to bring them under control in terms of aircraft, personnel and water drops. When a fire happens in similar terrain, vegetation and weather conditions, the previous data can be modelled to inform decisions based on specific data.

TracPlus systems are in use with aerial firefighting agencies they will despatch the lowest cost closest aircraft.

O'Hara said TracPlus is developing a model to show agencies the capability of an aircraft being despatched, including its fuel and retardant load, to make sure it is the most effective asset and that there isn't another aircraft a little further away with more fuel and retardant on board. The system allows operators and agencies to track where and when water was collected and drops were made, as well as how much water and retardant were used, something previously done manually by a crewmember writing it on a pad.

Some jurisdictions, such as Australia, New Zealand and California, replace or refund the costs of replacement when water is taken from private property, but without data determining the actual amount taken, that can result in a dispute between the land owner and the agency. O'Hara noted:"Previously, it was almost impossible to tell that, but using the new system they can see the exact amount that was farmed from this pond and was dropped on which property. It is metrics and data that simply were not available beforehand."

Another element to the FireFlyte platform that O'Hara is keen on is predictive pre-positioning, which is using data from past fires to predict where to position assets when similar conditions are expected. A scenario might be when a certain weather system is moving into an area where a previous fire occurred and the same type of fuel is on the ground. Based on previous data collected,

▶ **Bright orange Bambi Buckets are a familiar sight in wildfire operations.** SEI

worldwide, including CAL FIRE, Columbia Helicopters, Helicopter Express, Timberline Helicopters and NASA in the US. Australian users include McDermott Aviation, Kestrel, Microflite, NAFC and NSW Rural Fire Service, while in Europe Titan Aerial Firefighting, Pegasus and Avincis are TracPlus customers.

Bambi Buckets

For more than 40 years, helicopters have been fighting wildfires with a bright orange collapsible bucket slung underneath the aircraft, refilling it from water sources as low as 18in. The Bambi Bucket, manufactured by Canadian company SEI Industries, is so ubiquitous that the name has become the generic term for almost any underslung carrying system used in aerial firefighting.

While big aircraft and helicopters are often the stars of the show, there are many more everyday helicopters that answer the call when lives and property are threatened. These aircraft may only be firefighting for a few weeks a year, so collapsible buckets that are secured by a hook are a quick and cost effective tool for firefighting.

Wildfires in heavily wooded areas often mean the dense canopy makes it difficult for a tank drop to reach the fire and for the operator to accurately drop at the hot spot. In such situations, a bucket on a long line allows for a more concentrated and accurate drop. The ability perform a quick refill means helicopters can return to the fire with minimum delay.

Finding water sources during droughts or hot summers is a challenge in many areas and users in those situations can employ SEI's PowerFill technology. PowerFill allows users to fill their firefighting buckets in shallow water sources, such as rivers, creeks, stream beds and alpine meadows, where conventional dipping methods are not possible.

The Powerfill snorkel uses a pumping system that can use those shallow sources to fill the bucket at a rate of 420 US gal per minute.

The PowerFill snorkel can be installed in a matter of minutes by one person using the quick connection or the original bolt-on system. It is available for use with Bambi Buckets and Bambi MAX models ranging between 216 US gal to 425 US gall sizes. There are more than 40 models of Bambi Bucket to suit all types of helicopters, ranging in capacity from 72 US gal to 2,590 US gal in single- or multi-drop versions.

▲ **A Bambi Bucket allows operators to quickly transition between missions.** SEI

▲◄ **Avincis is the largest provider of emergency aerial services in Europe.** Avincis

▼ **An Erickson Air Crane fighting a major wildfire in Greece.** Erickson

When Size Matters

Firefighting expert Britt Coulson explains that as wildfires grow in frequency and intensity the best defence is to attack them quickly using large airtankers.

The firefighting world is a global community where operators, governments and agencies share resources in times of need, knowing that a favour done today will be returned in the future. It is a small world where people make the difference. For more than 65 years, the Coulson name has been front and centre in forestry operations and aerial firefighting.

That association started when Cliff Coulson founded Coulson Forest Products in 1960, the company taking a different turn in 1984 when Cliff's son Wayne created Coulson Aircrane in 1984. Large aircraft have been at the heart of the business since then. Today, Coulson is the world's largest operator of large fixed-wing and rotary airtankers, including

Boeing 737 FIRELINERs, C-130 Hercules, Chinook CH-47s and Sikorsky S-61s.

The Coulson Aviation Group remains a privately owned family firm based in Alberni, British Columbia, with operating subsidiaries worldwide, including Coulson Aviation Australia (CAA). The latter was established in 2010 and, in 2024, secured a ten-year

▼ **Coulson Aviation operates a fleet of 36 fixed-wing and rotary aircraft.**
Coulson

contract with the New South Wales Rural Fire service.

Coulson operates at every level of the aerial firefighting ecosystem, from air attack and intelligence to airtankers, helicopter co-ordination and helitankers. Having that vertical integration produces a clear understanding that one type or size of aircraft doesn't fit all situations, which is why Coulson has opted for a diversified fleet that includes four 737 FIRELINERs, six C-130 Hercules, five CH-47 Chinooks, four Sikorsky S-61s, two Sikorsky S-76s, six Bell-412s, one Bombardier Challenger, seven Cessna Citations and one King Air 350.

Coulson's distinctive aircraft can be seen fighting wildfires around the world, including in Canada, the US, South America and Australia. It is this global presence that gives Coulson Aviation president and chief operating officer Britt Coulson a clear picture of what's happening in global aerial firefighting and the new challenges emerging as climates change.

▲ Converting a 737 to a FIRELINER takes **60,000 man hours.**
Coulson

Emissions reduction

For the last six years, commercial aviation has been preoccupied with the issue of emissions reduction and how it can achieve the net-zero emissions targets most airlines have promised. The holy grail is developing clean propulsion systems, with an interim solution of using sustainable aviation fuel (SAF)

▲ Britt Coulson describes large airtankers as the big hammer in the toolbox when everything is burning. Coulson

▼ Highly trained and experienced crews operate globally. Coulson

from renewable feedstocks such as used cooking oil, food waste and other biomass. Progress has been slow and lacks sufficient investment to produce sufficient quantities of affordable SAF produced to replace fossil fuels.

Britt Coulson pointed out that capturing half the fires in Canada in an initial attack phase would outpace the switch to electric cars and that fire is always in the top five of carbon emissions. He believes that firefighting is low hanging fruit in comparison to what else is out there to reduce emissions: "In 2024, the wildfires in Canada put out more emissions than more than one-and-a-half times every vehicle in Canada combined. So when you look at electric cars and all the other things people are working on, fighting fire provides an amazing return on investment to protect the environment."

The message is that fire is not a natural disaster and that there needs to be a shift in thinking to understand That the majority of fire is caused by humans. Investing more in mitigating fire is one of the largest positive impacts society could have on reducing emissions and protecting the environment.

The world has less than 60 large firefighting airtankers and the harsh truth is that wildfires are shifting to be a year-round event and there

lose a significant number of lives and burn hundreds of billions of dollars of real estate and not have something change. It happened in Lahaina (Hawaii) and now it has happened again in California, so is it worth losing lives and hundreds of billions of dollars compared to the relatively low investment of having additional crew and aircraft all year round that could have minimised the impact?"

On the surface, a change like that seems manageable, but Britt points out there are so few large airtankers and even fewer large helitankers in the world, so demand outstrips supply. That balance has also been upset by uncertainty and disruptions in shipping large

helicopters by sea, which has turned a once predicable logistics chain into a lottery. Coulson said: "With the variability of the fire season extending, time for maintenance shrinking and the uncertain shipping schedule, it became harder to move the rotary wing around to the point that we don't do it anymore. We see it converging into a single point now of everyone needing their own assets and sharing the large airtankers, which can fly around the world quickly in a time of need."

Australian connection

The shift is happening with governments like New South Wales in Australia purchasing their own

are not enough aircraft to meet that change. Getting to a fire in its early stages and dumping large loads of water and retardant from a C-130, 737 FIRELINER or a Chinook helicopter is the best defence available, which is the world Coulson Aviation inhabits.

Paradigm shift

The major challenge facing the aerial firefighting industry is the growing realisation there are not enough large aircraft to sustain the traditional model of moving assets around the world to match fire seasons. The concept of definable fire seasons is rapidly fading, as evidenced by the Los Angeles fires in early 2025, and governments now want the large aircraft to arrive earlier and stay later.

Britt explained: "It's a big paradigm shift, because you don't

◄ **Coulson 737 FIRELINERS will be firefighting in Chile.** Coulson

▼ **Coulson pioneered night firefighting with night-vision goggles.** Coulson

▲ Coulson is fostering the next generation of aviation technicians. Coulson

▼ With a fleet of five Chinooks, Coulson has significant assets to hand. Coulson

the fleet. The RFS fleets includes a 737 FIRELINER, a CH-47 Chinook, six Bell 412s, a Beechcraft Super King Air and two Cessna Citations.

CAA is doing far more than operating firefighting aircraft as it is investing in the future of Australian aviation by primarily hiring local pilots and technicians. The company is expanding an apprenticeship programme to develop the next generation of aviation talent in New South Wales. A minimum of two mechanical apprentices are part of the aviation team at any time, providing them with the opportunity to gain hands-on experience with the diverse range of firefighting aircraft.

Coulson explained what the project was trying to achieve: "We are working with NSW schools in Richmond to partner with them on the training side and trying to foster that new generation of pilots and mechanics that is not entirely for airlines. There's a lot of other amazing careers in aviation that are not airline-based that we are really highlighting."

The NSW 737 FIRELINER is based at RAAF Base Richmond, 40 miles west of Sydney, which is also home the RAAF's C-130J Hercules aircraft squadron. From there, it can reach any location in New South Wales within one hour and can also operate from some regional

firefighting fleet and lending them out for two to three months per year to offset their costs. The large airtankers are ideal for this as, within a few hours, the internal tank can be removed and the aircraft used for other missions, such as flood relief and evacuations.

In 2024, CAA secured a ten-year contract with the the New South Wales Rural Fire Service (RFS) to manage, operate and maintain its fleet of 11 aircraft. The contract is valued at £192m and continues a previous five-year contract where Coulson manged the majority of airports. The aircraft is named *Marie Bashir* after a former governor of NSW and operates with a crew of two pilots. It has a cruise speed of 469kt, typically flies at an altitude of 35,000ft and needs a runway length of 6,430ft. It joined the RFS fleet in 2019 and has been deployed each year internationally to assist in global firefighting efforts.

737 FIRELINERs

Coulson Aviation acquires Boeing 737s and converts them in-house to 737 FIRELINER airtankers, but with the modifications taking about 60,000 man hours it is limited to converting just two per year. The company is building a new facility to add to its US base which means it will be able to increase 737 FIRELINER output in future years. Britt said: "If we are going to be moving firefighters from Sydney to Perth, the only aircraft that can do that is the 737. It can load 66 firefighters, fly them to Perth and offload them while the aircraft is loading retardant and, in less than half-an-hour, both the firefighters and the 737 FIRELINER are heading to the fire."

One of the reasons Coulson went with the Boeing 737 was because it is a lower slung aeroplane compared to Airbus

▲ Chinook CH-47s are a potent weapon for fighting wildfires. Coulson

A319 and 320 family jets. That is important because many of the tanker bases and airports from which the company operates do not have air stairs or the type of infrastructure needed to support the other platforms.

The Boeing 737 has an OEM forward air stair system that folds up into a closet in the main cabin just below the forward entrance door. The lower aircraft also allows for easy access to the cargo pit and retardant fill ports for the loading crews without using a ladder, which increases ground safety and adds to the usability of the aircraft on firefighting missions in remote areas.

Britt also said that the company prefers to use Boeing aircraft, such as the earlier 737/737NGs, rather than an airframe with a fly-by-wire system, such as the Airbus A320. The reasoning is that the more robust,

heavy-duty design is a better fit for the types of flying associated with firefighting, which puts a different type of strain on the aircraft to traditional commercial operation: "We're putting more cycles on them, so it's more fatiguing on the aircraft and we're down low in much gustier environments than the aircraft's design envelope. Having a strong airframe that has been developed and refined over decades is a huge value for our mission profile and leads to a higher margin to safety, so it was a much safer choice."

Initially, Coulson converted 737-300s, but in 2024 it took delivery of its first 737-700NG (next generation) variant, part of the same family as the popular 737-800s. The 737-700NG will increase payload to 5000 US gallons, a gain of around 25% compared to the current FIRELINER.

▼ RADS-XXL is the world's highest capacity system holding 4,000 US gallons. Coulson

▲ Coulson pilots operate missions in all conditions 24/7.
Coulson

▼ Sikorsky S61 and Chinook CH-47 helitankers are a potent pairing.
Coulson

The initial 737-700NG arrived in May 2024 and is the first of ten former Southwest Airlines airframes to be repurposed under Coulson's Next Gen FIRELINER programme. The company expects to have it ready for the 2027 North American fire season.

Adding C-130H capacity

Coulson is certainly doing more than anyone to add more large airtankers into the global pool, but sourcing legacy aircraft is not easy and it takes a long time for them to modified and ready to assume firefighting duties. In April 2025, the company announced that it had acquired four C-130Hs that had previously served with the Royal New Zealand Air Force for conversion to firefighting operations. These will head to Coulson's base in Thermal, California, to be modified and have various systems upgraded. They will be fitted with Coulson's proprietary RADS-XXL tank system, which can hold up to 4,000 US gallons – the world's highest capacity, highest flow rate large airtanker system.

Britt commented: "These aircraft continue to enhance our ability to respond rapidly and effectively to wildfires and other natural disasters around the world,-saving lives, protecting communities and safeguarding critical natural and economic resources. With the four additional C-130Hs in our fleet we're reaffirming our commitment to lead the industry with the most capable, high performance large airtankers out there."

The sale and transfer of C-130s is tightly controlled by the US government due to the aircraft's military capability and Coulson, which is already the largest civilian operator of the type, is now the ninth largest operator of military C-130s worldwide. The upside is that buying C-130s from sovereign air forces means they have usually been well maintained and have many years of firefighting service ahead.

On the subject of using these large aircraft in a new role, Britt said the platforms it has chosen are the only aircraft where the series are still in production. This is important for sustainability, supply chain and to assure that the aircraft are still being supported by the original equipment manufacturers: "Having the ability to phone the OEM when you need help is very important to us and the fact that they are major OEMs that are still in business is a huge benefit. So Boeing supports the 737, Lockheed supports the C-130 and Sikorsky supports their aircraft."

The toolbox

Emergency operators are always talking about aircraft as just another tool in the toolbox. The toolbox needs to fit the mission and not the other way round. On one occasion, an agency contracted a Dash 8-Q400 aircraft to reduce costs, but subsequently found that it needed four Q400 drops to equal what the C-130 could do in one drop, which was primarily due to a less efficient tank design on the smaller aircraft.

Britt explained: "When we're responding to a wildfire event, we could dispatch a fleet of smaller aircraft, like Bell 412s, but it's going to take multiple aircraft significantly longer to deliver the same volume as one CH-47, so why take the increased risk, flight time and fuel burn? There's a compromise of large assets versus medium and smaller assets. Our diverse fleet allows customers to pick the right aircraft for the job."

Extreme fire weather – as was experienced in California in early 2025 – can only be effectively addressed from the air using large airtankers. While medium and small sized aircraft can make a difference when conditions suit, they are no match for the ferocious fires that are becoming more common around the world: "Southern California during Santa Anna wind events is like the Super Bowl of firefighting, where fire danger is at its highest and even a 4,000 gallon payload out of a C-130 may not hit the ground. So a 500 gallon drop out of single engine airtanker or smaller helicopter just doesn't get the job done. When push comes to shove, on the highest of fire danger days, you don't see the small aircraft out there."

Night shift

Coulson was the first private company to do night-firefighting, launched in the Australian state of Victoria along with local operator Kestrel joining in with a Bell 412. Britt said that aerial firefighting is much more efficient at night because the temperature goes down, the humidity goes up and typically there is less wind.

There are also fewer aircraft operating at night, which leads to a quieter and more sterile radio environment than during the hustle and bustle of the day.

Run descriptions are much easier at night because, rather than trying to describe a target over a congested radio, pilots can follow a laser beam and drop their load more accurately.

Britt added: "The risks increase at night, so you want to have your most capable aircraft out there and we feel those aircraft should be limited to firebombing Type 1s, such as the S-61 or CH-47 down at low level, as they provide the best return versus risk. When you are low level, that's where the risk is highest, so you want the optimal aircraft that generates the most value."

Supporting Chile

In 2024, Coulson announced that it had won an additional large airtanker contract with Chile's National Forest Corporation (CONAF) solidifying itself as the

▲ Arrival of the C-130 airtankers is always a welcome sight. Coulson

▼ Loading tanks quickly is vital in aerial firefighting. Coulson

▲ Coulson has a highly skilled design and engineering operation. Coulson

▼ Reliable water sources can be scarce in many regions. Coulson

sole provider of large airtankers in the South American country. Coulson has been operating in Chile since 2021 and has become Chile's leading provider of integrated large aerial firefighting services. Its strategic partnership with local emergency services provider BRYSA was instrumental in securing the contract. This expanded Coulson's ongoing support of firefighting in Chile using a diverse suite of aircraft, including the Boeing 737 FIRELINER, C-130 Hercules and Citation air attack aircraft.

Introducing the 737 FIRELINER is a significant boost to CONAF's aerial firefighting fleet as it will provide enhanced coverage and allow rapid response to suppress fires across the challenging terrain of Chile.

The Citation 550 air attack lead is used to co-ordinate the aircraft to increase safety. The fast, agile jet stays above all firefighting and other aircraft to allow its crew to direct aircraft, provide safe separation and increase overall efficiency. Coulson is the only aerial firefighting company operating large airtankers with air attack lead aircraft internationally.

Future outlook

Britt strongly believes that adding more large airtankers is the way to tackle the issues of seasonality, fire suppression and emissions reduction, but he also acknowledges an conflict between supply and demand. He said that the industry needs to be more proactive about the issues it is facing because putting things off will always cost more in the end: "I'll point to New South Wales as they are a great example of forward thinking and being ahead of the curve, because they

have invested and secured their future by purchasing their own large airtanker and helitanker

before any other countries had done this. These same aircraft are now going for 25% more than what NSW paid and we are talking to multiple countries about this same model going forward as they desire to build their own sovereign capability."

With large aircraft scarce and demand rising, the costs are bound to increase and there will be countries that will not be able to afford to buy or lease the most effective assets. The net result is that, without proper planning,

these agencies will be limited to smaller and less effective aircraft. Britt emphasised: "With fire behaviour escalating year after year and so few large airtankers and helitankers available globally, it's clear the industry needs to evolve. These aircraft are just one tool in the firefighting toolbox, but when everything is burning, they're the big hammer. We're building the next generation of aerial firefighting to be faster, smarter, and ready for what's coming."

▲ Firefighting at night is a very effective tactic.
Coulson

▼ Britt Coulson said having a strong airframe is critical.
Coulson

THE DESTINATION FOR AVIATION ENTHUSIASTS

Radical
Solutions

With longer fire seasons, agencies worldwide are battling to find the tankers they need. Four new aircraft promise a revolutionary future.

Aerial firefighting is an expensive, risky and complex business where there are roles for all sizes of rotary and fixed-wing aircraft, many of which can remove their water tanks and be deployed on other missions when fire seasons abate.

However, there is no disputing that the prime firefighting stars are the heavy lift aircraft, particularly the C-130 tankers and big helicopters such as the Erikson Air Crane, Columbia Chinook and Sikorsky Black Hawk. It's not surprising to see decades-old helicopters at the forefront of these battles, but their uniqueness means that there is only a finite supply and there are simply not enough to go around.

These assets are often owned by global operators who move them worldwide as seasons change, tracing a well-flown path between the US, Australia and Europe, followed by maintenance and crew training. However, ever-longer fire seasons have exposed the lack of sufficient large tankers as local authorities and agencies request they stay in their regions for longer, disrupting the movement of aircraft on a seasonal basis.

With demand rising and supply falling, four organisations stepped forward in 2025 with innovative plans for new firefighting aircraft, including an Italian firm offering a clean-sheet design for an amphibious turboprop. The concepts were unveiled in France at Aerial Fire Fighting Europe 2025 to an audience of operators, governments, fire agencies, industry bodies and aerospace manufacturers.

Apart from the new Italian aircraft, the other three companies have adopted popular turboprop platforms using the De Havilland Dash 8 and ATR 72 aircraft. Both are proven performers and highly regarded for their reliability and durability in challenging environments, with the added advantage of their having established service networks worldwide.

Italian innovation

It is not often that clean-sheet design aircraft are announced, let alone actually make it through production and launch, as evidenced by the numerous eVTOL products that have been unveiled with much fanfare in recent years. From its Italian base, 19-01 Holding is set to redefine aerial firefighting with its new WF-X Waterfall turboprop, an amphibious Type-1 large tanker.

The Waterfall is a multi-role platform with a range of 2,600nm, which makes it ideal for missions including firefighting, search and rescue, maritime surveillance, aeromedical support, emergency evacuation and passenger and cargo services. Former airline pilot and aviation consultant Renato Sacchetti is the founder and CEO of 19-01 Holding and has been secretly working on the project for more than 14 years.

Sacchetti believes the advantages of a clean-sheet design far outweigh those associated with converting an existing aircraft, despite all of the challenges with designing, building and certifying a totally new airframe. He said: "Many people believe it is easier to adapt an existing aircraft, but that's not the case because it involves lots of compromises. It depends on whether you want to start from something you already have and try to find a different market, but if you take the customer need first then you have to go for a clean-sheet design. There's no other way."

Sacchetti started the project in 2011, when he recognised the limitations of existing and ageing aircraft like the Canadair CL-215/415, which form the backbone of many firefighting operators in Canada and Europe. However, he knew that designing an aircraft solely for firefighting would not be commercially viable, so the Waterfall was devised to be a multi-role aircraft that could be converted to other missions in less than three hours. He explained: "The Canadair was made back in 1969, does not fly at night, is only for firefighting and, if I'm not wrong, went out of production in 2015. We are still at the first generation in firefighting aircraft, so we designed something that was modern, could fly at night in all conditions and be used for several missions."

In its firefighting mode, the Type-1 large tanker will have a maximum take-off weight of 30 tonnes, with the capacity to carry up to 12 tonnes of water and retardants, which is more than a Boeing 737, BAe-146 and C-130 fitted with MAFFS II (modular airborne firefighting system – self-contained units that can be loaded onto military cargo transport C-130 Hercules and Embraer C-390 aircraft).

▼ **Positive Aviation is developing the FF72 on a Dash 8 platform.**
Positive Aviation

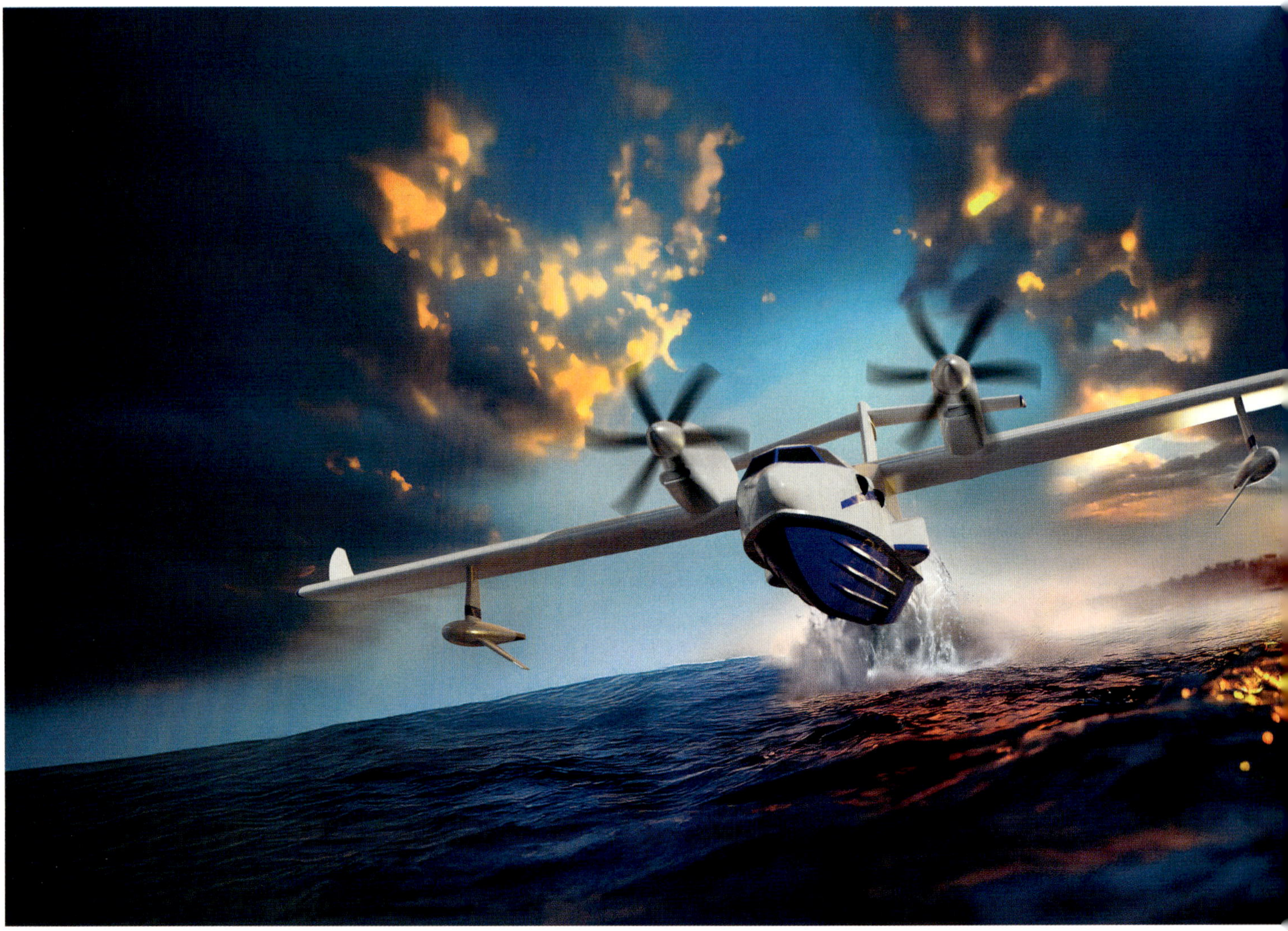

A significant advantage of the Waterfall over other large tankers is that it refills its tanks inflight directly from a body of water using a scooper mechanism to quickly return to the fire, whereas other large tankers need to land to refill their tanks. This capability to be back on station repeatedly is vital given that it usually takes more than a single tank drop to fully extinguish a raging wildfire.

It has taken some years for aerial firefighting at night to be approved and gain acceptance, but more and more agencies worldwide are employing these expensive assets when the conditions make them more effective. At night, temperatures, humidity and wind strength are usually lower, which optimises the effectiveness of aircraft drops.

The Waterfall will be fully fitted for night-firefighting, with cockpit and lighting equipment compatible with night-vision goggles, while 360° enhanced vision is obtained by integrating specialised infrared (IR) cameras with a high-performance electro-optical (EO) turret.

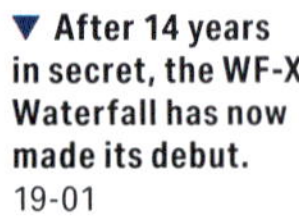
▲ The WF-X Waterfall is a clean-sheet design amphibious scooper turboprop. 19-01

▼ After 14 years in secret, the WF-X Waterfall has now made its debut. 19-01

Dropping water and retardants at low levels is potentially hazardous, so to improve safety the Waterfall crew wear devices that integrate data from a sense-and-avoid system that supports the detection of crossing electrical cables or eventual mid-air obstacles.

Sacchetti is also keen to highlight the technology that puts the Waterfall at the centre of a system of systems that include satellites, drones, ground crews and controllers. Fire zones are usually extremely challenging to navigate for pilots who need to be 100% accurate with their drops, so 19-01 has implemented technology to make that safer and more effective: "We have an infrared target under the wing that spots the warmest part of the fire and an algorithm for the trajectory of the water and you have data from the aircraft giving speed, heading, altitude, wind and so on. It combines everything and the algorithm opens the door exactly when the moment is right so the pilot just flies the corridor in a safe way."

With its funding in place, 19-01 Holding is now in the pre-production phase after finalising the aircraft's specifications in 2021, and with its supply chain partners locked down, a new production site has been selected. The first Waterfall prototype is being manufactured and it is expected to take its first flight in 2028 and gain regulatory certification by the end of 2030.

Positive alternative

Toulouse Blagnac Airport in south-western France is the home of Airbus and ATR, the world's leading manufacturer of new-generation passenger turboprop aircraft up to 78 seats. Those two aerospace leaders now have a new neighbour, Positive Aviation, which is developing its FF72 medium tanker aircraft from new headquarters at the airport.

The team behind Positive Aviation include former senior executives from the joint venture partners of ATR, Airbus and Leonardo, who have been quietly developing the FF72 concept for more than two years. The team saw the need for a modern, reliable and affordably

▲ **Filling its tanks using scoopers allows the WF-X to deliver more drops.**
19-01

◀ **WF-X Waterfall is a multi-mission aircraft with a 2,600nm range.**
19-01

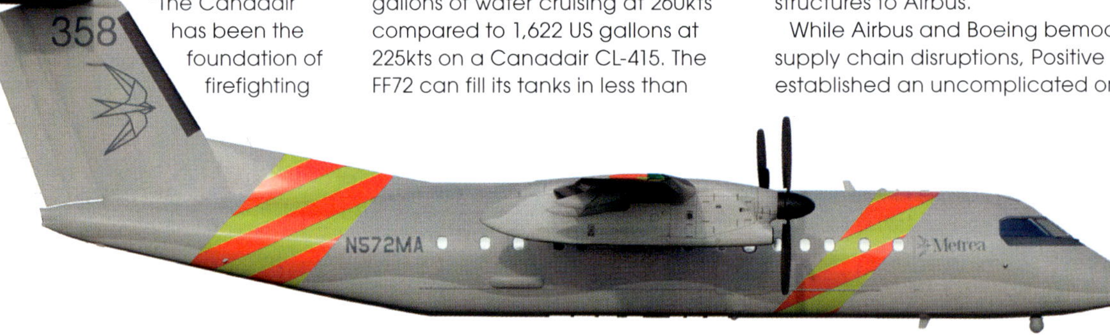

priced tanker to replace ageing platforms and meet the increasing demand for firefighting aircraft.

Positive was founded on the principle that authorities can only effectively safeguard people, property and nature when equipped with the rights tools, and the iconic Canadair Super Scooper no longer meets the standards required today. Co-Founder Raoudha Jammoussi said the first option considered was to use an Airbus A319 with a fixed tank, but when that was presented to the European agencies they quickly determined that any new aircraft needed to refill using water scoops, not by returning to an airfield.

Aircraft choice is heavily dependent on the proximity of water fills in different regions, which is why countries around the Mediterranean have based their systems around scooping, whereas Australia and the US use aircraft like the 737 and C-130 Hercules that return to base for refilling.

Jammoussi explained: "The Canadair has been the foundation of firefighting in Europe because the number of rotations that are possible between the water fills - a lake, sea or river - and the fire are so quick that the fire does not have time to heat up again. We needed to replace a scooper with a scooper because using a fixed tank was a huge change to the operation."

Positive then looked to ATR and developed a design that converted a new or used ATR 72 into a FF72, which has a similar footprint to the Canadair but can carry 2,113 US gallons of water cruising at 260kts compared to 1,622 US gallons at 225kts on a Canadair CL-415. The FF72 can fill its tanks in less than 12 secs and empty them in 1.2 secs and has interchangeable floats that ensure a quick return to service if damaged.

The high wing and engine mounts make the ATR 72 ideal for water scooping, minimising potential damage and corrosion, and the landing gear is integrated with the floats. The floats are made by Multiplast, a French company focused on high-tech composite multi- and mono-hull boat construction that also supplies structures to Airbus.

While Airbus and Boeing bemoan supply chain disruptions, Positive has established an uncomplicated one

of its own, with new aircraft coming from ATR in Toulouse, the floats from Multiplast and the modification work undertaken by ARTS Solutions, also based at Toulouse Airport.

With more than 1,000 ATR aircraft in service, there is a steady stream of used airframes being replaced with new ones and buyers of the FF72 have the choice of using a new or used aircraft. Modifying a new or refurbished aircraft will take four months, with two months for structural reinforcements and installation, one month for systems installation and another month for testing and delivery.

Operators of the FF72 have easy access to spare parts and are supported by the existing global ATR service network. The launch customeris US operator Bridger Aerospace, which has signed a memorandum of understanding to purchase ten FF72s. with options for a further ten. Bridger will also be the exclusive US representative of Positive Aviation for sales, support, spare parts, float repair and FF72 customisation and delivery.

The aviation pedigree of the Positive Aviation founders shows through in all facets of this new venture, including the need to provide support, service and training to a global fleet. In line with its social objectives, Positive wants to make the FF72 an affordable platform for nations that struggle to afford or justify the cost of tanker aircraft. It has an entry price of around €80 million. To ease that burden, a new build aircraft will cost €40m or €32m if a secondhand ATR 72 is used.

The FF72 was unveiled in March 2025 and Positive said the first demonstrator aircraft is on track for its maiden flight in 2026, with certification and entry into service by the end of 2028. The plan is to produce six aircraft in 2029

▲ **FIRESWIFT has a water tank capacity of 1,500galUS.** Metrea

◀ **The WF-X is expected to make its maiden flight in 2028.** 19-01

and quickly ramp up to 12 per year in 2030 and beyond.

FIRESWIFT emerges

From its headquarters in the US, Metrea works with national security partners across multiple domains and solutions, including aerial refuelling, electronic warfare, communications, advanced simulation and airborne and space based intelligence, surveillance and reconnaissance missions. It operates the world's largest fleet of privately

owned tanker aircraft and has leveraged that capability to develop its new FIRESWIFT firefighting platform. FIRESWIFT was unveiled at Aerial Fire Fighting Europe 2025, where it showcased the aircraft's advanced precision drop capabilities and cutting edge surveillance and communications technologies.

The twin turboprop FIRESWIFT DHC-8-300AFF is converted from a De Havilland Dash 8-300, a tried and trusted aircraft with a long history of operations in remote areas and

▼ **Metrea has based the FIRESWIFT on a Dash 8-300.** Metrea

▲ Positive Aviation is developing the FF72 in France.
Positive Aviation

▶ High wings and engines make the FF72 ideal for water scooping.
Positive Aviation

▼ US operator Bridger Aerospace is the FF72 launch customer.
Positive Aviation

challenging environments. With the capacity to carry 1,500 US gallons of water, it is classified as a Type-III medium tanker, smaller than the Type-II based on the Dash 8-400 model, which has the capacity for 2,640 US gallons.

The FIRESWIFT has been in development since 2022 and Metrea's aerial firefighting capabilities lead Ryan Becker said the modifications to the Dash 8-300 are significant form a structural standpoint as the mission and load spectrum of the aircraft is changing.

During the COVID-19 pandemic there was a rush to convert older passenger aircraft, including turboprops, into freighters and the process of tanker conversions is well known and reliable. Becker said the FIRESWIFT is going through the same certification process that all air tankers have encountered over the last 15 years. He explained there are a lot of factors that make a compelling case for the Dash 8-300 as a medium air tanker and that there's

a disincentive among the majority of countries with a wildfire problems to make that large an investment in large expensive single-use tools: "The FIRESWIFT is a medium tanker with a smaller payload, but it has great short field capabilities, great operating economics and the size to perform multiple missions."

The aircraft is fitted with EO/IR full motion video and is the only

special mission Dash 8 aircraft equipped with Starlink connectivity, which provides high-performance low-cost beyond-line-of-sight communications. It is also well equipped for night-firefighting, with a WESCAM MX-15 EO/IR turret under the aircraft. Such sophisticated tracking systems ensure the aircraft is well suited to maritime surveillance, search and rescue and similar emergency operations night and day in all weather conditions.

Becker said: "What we're aiming for with FIRESWIFT is to put the human in the loop at the point of action, so they have all of the inputs necessary to make those best decisions, and also provide them with the tools that let them get a better picture than what is available right now, such as on-the-ly fire growth prediction based on the measured inputs at the location."

The aircraft is on track to make its flying debut with demonstrations in summer 2025, although no timeline

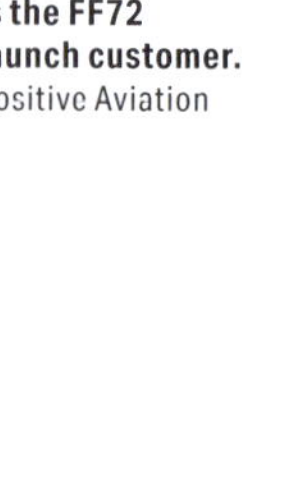

▲ FF72 buyers can choose from new or used ATR72 aircraft.
Positive Aviation

to certification or entry into service is yet available. The initial FIRESWIFT demonstrations will include the EO/IR capability and a functioning drop system that will make a series of low passes with drops in a safe area.

Becker said he prefers to see observers walk through the drop area after the demonstration so they can get their feet wet and gain a better understanding of the amount of water that hit the ground: "That's what the firefighters really care about, not what the plane looks like when it is flying."

One to watch

The fourth new entrant is the Kepplair KE-72, a versatile Type-II air tanker that also operates as a cargo transport aircraft when not on firefighting missions. It is based on the ATR 72 platform and is designed to carry two tanks with a total capacity of 1,981 gallons or 8.5 tonnes of freight with the tanks removed. It is being developed by Kepplair Evolution with the aim of helping as many countries as possible to reduce the amount of land burned, while minimising the cost of aerial firefighting in natural areas and optimising the possible missions flown.

It has a high rotation speed of 318kts and can be configured for medevac missions, enabling up to six casualties on stretchers to be transported in complete safety, along with a secure ventilation and electrical system.

The company said it completed its pre-design review in March 2025 and the first KE-72 prototypes would be manufactured between March 2026 and 2027. The plan is to launch the first flight between July and December 2027, with the initial deliveries and entry into service in 2028.

◄ Water scoopers are popular in European firefighting.
Positive Aviation

▼ Kepplair is aiming to launch the KE-72 in 2028. Kepplair

Flying the
Doctors

▼ **RFDS pilot Tamlyn Gresser said learning from experienced captains is invaluable.** RFDS

Australia's Royal Flying Doctor Service is one of the largest and most comprehensive aeromedical organisations in the world and with a territory of nearly three million square miles it probably has the biggest waiting room as well.

Using a fleet of 81 fixed-wing and rotary aircraft, the Royal Flying Doctor Service (RFDS) provided essential primary healthcare, emergency aeromedical and telehealth services to more than 340,000 patients in 2024, including 33,000 transported by an aeromedical aircraft.

Its genesis was in July 1917 when an outback stockman suffered massive internal injuries after his horse fell on him in a cattle stampede in the far north of Western Australia. He endured a 50-mile ride on a dray over a rough track to the nearest settlement, where the local postmaster had to perform emergency surgery with the help of morse code, a penknife and some morphine.

With the man at death's door, a doctor 1,800 miles away in Perth sent telegraph instructions to repair a ruptured bladder and, although the operation was a success, the stockman later died from malaria while a doctor spent a week journeying to the scene. The Reverend John Flynn was deeply

Located 250 miles northwest of Sydney is the Dubbo base, which is home to the RFDS Visitor Experience and an operational facility providing 24/7 aeromedical retrieval and patient transfers using King Air turboprops. It also houses a flight training simulator, training facilities for doctors and nurses, an operations control centre and an engineering facility.

One of the King Air pilots working from the Dubbo base is Tamlyn Gresser, whose love of flying was ignited in her student days by a work experience assignment at the RFDS base in Broken Hill. After school, she followed that dream by obtaining a pilot's licence and spending a few years flying all over Australia doing surveying, charter and freight jobs before joining the RFDS in 2022.

To give a first-hand insight into the life of an emergency aeromedical pilot she shared some of her experiences, including how the role differs from a commercial pilot and why the King Air is so well suited to the various RFDS missions across Australia. To begin that conversation she explained why she loves the job: "I get so much more meaning out of what I am doing every day than from my previous roles, which weren't as meaningful. Often you're meeting people on the worst day of their life and you are playing a part in getting them access to the healthcare they need and that's a huge privilege, although it comes with a lot more pressure."

Making up around half of the fleet, the King Air twin engine turboprops are the backbone of the service where their high speed and long range make them an ideal aircraft for the mix of

▲ The RFDS services distant sites across Australia. RFDS

◀ King Air B200s are the backbone of the RFDS fleet. RFDS

▼ The de Havilland Dragon was an early RFDS aircraft. RFDS

affected by the death and turned his concern into a vision to provide a mantle of safety for people in the outback.

In May 1918, pilot Arthur Affleck took off from the outback Queensland town of Cloncurry for Julia Creek in Flynn's first flying ambulance. The de Havilland DH.50 was leased from the new Longreach-based bush airline, the Queensland and Northern Territory Aerial Services, now known as QANTAS.

Pilot's perspective

Aircraft are an integral part of the not-for-profit service and the national fleet operates across the country from 23 widely dispersed bases on a 24/7 basis. The fleet includes Pilatus PC-12, King Air B200/B350 and Beechcraft King Air 360CHW turboprops, Pilatus PC-24 jets and Airbus EC-145 helicopters, all of which are tailored to the needs of the RFDS.

FLYING THE DOCTORS

cross-country and urban flying. They are flown by a single pilot and a flight nurse is usually on board every flight, with a doctor aboard depending on the severity of the situation.

The cabin is typically fitted with three seats and two stretcher beds that can be configured to suit the mission or allow for other patients, relatives or specialist medical staff. The RFDS aircraft have been modified to replace the standard passenger door with a large cargo door to facilitate easy patient loading and unloading.

There are two main types of cabin layouts with some aircraft being configured for clinics or aeromedical services, while others have a hybrid configuration that can be changed to either mode or are a half-half type. They have a patient-loading device capable of loading 340kg into the aircraft with just two people assisting, including stretcher and other ancillary equipment.

The fit-outs are conducted by Australian company Total Aerospace Solutions, which in 2008 designed, manufactured and installed a modular aeromedical fit-out for King Air B200s. They allow for a dazzling array of medical and care equipment and closely resemble the inside of a road ambulance, with custom medical cabinets, electrical outlets and aeromedical seats with an integrated intercom switch panel in the armrest.

The aircraft are pressurised to safely transport patients critically sensitive to pressure changes and it also allows the King Airs to operate at higher altitudes to avoid turbulence or bad weather. The aircraft have an additional battery to provide medical power, a medical oxygen and suction system and a communication system between the cockpit and the cabin medical staff.

"You work so closely with the medical teams that you start to pick up on cues when something is not going well down back and they don't even have to really say anything but you just know what's going on," added Gresser. "So, when you combine that with terrible weather that means you can't get into a destination then that pressure is really unique to this kind of work."

The King Air has a two-person cockpit, but RFDS and many other

▲ King Airs have the speed, range and reliability demanded by RFDS missions.
RFDS

◀ Two Airbus EC-145s are operated in a partnership between the RFDS and Fortesque Metals.
RFDS

operators operate it with a single pilot, which heightens the load in challenging weather or critical medical missions. A flight can be on its way to a call and be diverted to higher priority cases or to another destination depending on the patient's condition or the weather.

There are also the challenges of landing on all conceivable types of runways at night in remote regions that you have not previously seen, while also flying the aircraft and communicating with multiple sources on the ground. It can, and often is, an intense workload

for a single pilot, who needs to be aware of what is happening in the cabin – Gresser said these pressures are what sets it apart from commercial flying.

"This doesn't happen all the time, but sometimes we can be contacted via the phone from the ambulance centre and if the nurse is really busy and it's appropriate I can take the call and be talking to them as well. Or in cases when they can't reach us, I've actually had air traffic control come on and give me an instruction about a diversion that's needed."

The Dubbo base is part of the South Eastern Section, which covers the state of New South Wales, but its aircraft can also travel into Queensland, Victoria or South Australia depending on the situation, particularly when operating patient transfer flights.

With a range nearing 1,700 miles, the King Air 200s can easily accommodate these longer flights, but most are generally around a two-hour duration.

Given the wide diversity and length of runways in remote regions, the aeroplanes may not always take off with full tanks as a runway may not be able to handle the full fuel load. "The King Airs can get into a lot of the 1,000m (3,300ft) strips out in the countryside, but they are also quick enough to get people around the place in a timely fashion while being fun to fly," Gresser said.

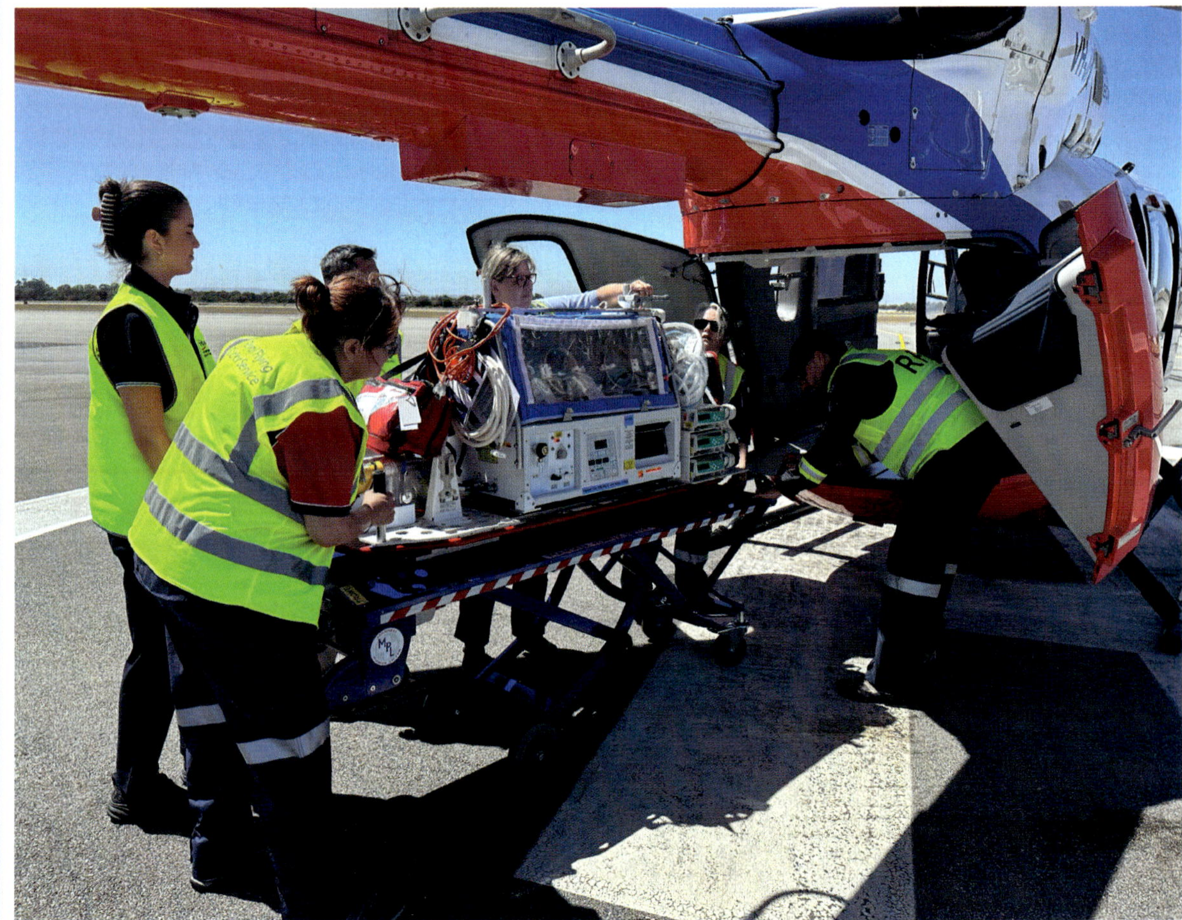

Patient transfers are a large part of the schedule and these often require picking up patients in rural and remote regions to transfer them to major cities for specialist treatment and then returning them home. For Gresser, these involve bringing patients to Dubbo or operating a flight into a capital city airport, which is something she enjoys: "A lot of our work is doing transport and for more critical cases we can take them to Adelaide or Sydney, where we use Mascot (Kingsford Smith Airport). In small airports we need to slow down, but when you're on the ILS in Sydney they want us to speed up to keep up with the jets, although if it's a medevac situation we get priority and they give us a lot of help."

The uniqueness of the role means that new pilots go through a rigorous training programme when they join the Royal Flying Doctor Service that ensures they can successfully transition from the commercial flying environment. Gresser said that for obvious reasons the requirements to join the service are quite high, but that's matched by the amount of time, skill and effort put in during the RFDS training process.

Speaking about her experience, Gresser said she was put with a training captain for 140 hours of flying in command under supervision, which she found to be a contrast to what happens in many commercial outfits that are often keen to get new hires checked to line as soon as possible: "I found the opposite at the RFDS where they really wanted to hone in on those skills and spending so much time with a check captain

who's had years of experience was so valuable," she said. "It's what gives me the confidence and the procedures to actually be able to carry out this work really safely and competently.

"As a single pilot, things can suddenly go wrong and it's just about having someone else there to give you the practical measures of how to go about that and the experience of learning from someone else who's handled that before. That experience is just so invaluable."

As the interview drew to a close, Gresser said some pilots would probably not enjoy the role, but most of the RFDS pilots just love what they do, which she attributes to the "really rewarding" nature of the role: "When someone is an organ donor recipient and they finally get the call that the organ has come in for us to be able to take them to where they are going to receive, that is really, really special. A lot of our guys really do it for the love of it and it's very rewarding."

Today's aircraft

In 2025, the national fleet contained 81 aircraft, including 34 Pilatus PC-12s, ten King Air B300s, 30 King Air B200s and one King Air BB360; it also operates four Pilatus PC-24 jets and two EC145 helicopters in partnership with Fortesque Metals

▲ Pilots and crew are often in remote regions. RFDS

▼ Landings on short, unpaved runways are all in day's work. RFDS

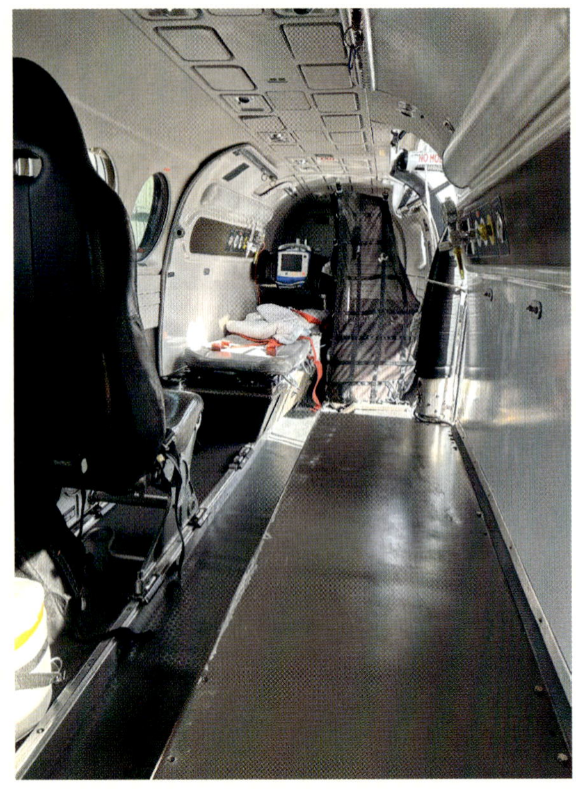

▲ Cabins are fitted out with aeromedical kits in Australia.
RFDS

▼ The service transports patients from remote regions to big city care.
Paul Sadler

The PC-12 has a maximum speed of 280kts, a range of 1,795 miles and a maximum altitude of 30,000ft. The cabin is 5ft wide, 15ft long and 57in high, making it an excellent all-rounder in terms of capacity, amenity, speed, range and performance for the parts of Australia in which it operates.

The instrumentation on the Pilatus PC-12 includes state-of-the-art Enhanced Ground Proximity Warning and Advisory Systems Navigation systems, including GPS and the standard equipment to display data from ground-based navigational aids. It is powered by a single Pratt & Whitney Canada PT6A-67B turboprop engine.

The cabin is configured for single pilot operations in all weather conditions day and night and the front door allows the pilots to conduct pre-flight external inspections and enter the aircraft without disturbing the patients and medical crew in the rear. A flight nurse is usually on board, accompanied by a doctor when a patient is seriously ill.

The majority of the King Airs are B200 types that have a top speed of 278kts, a range of 1,680 miles and a ceiling of 35,000ft. The King Air B300/350s are quicker at 305kts with a range of 1,865 miles and ceiling of 35,000ft while the BB360 is the fastest and farthest at 312kts with a range of 2,080 miles and a maximum altitude of 35,000ft.

Group, a leading Australian resources company based in Western Australia.

The fixed wing fleet is dispersed across the nation with the Pilatus PC-12 and PC 24 used in South Australia, Western Australia and the Northen Territory, the King Air B350 and B200 in Queensland, New South Wales, Victoria and Tasmania and the Beechcraft 360 in Queensland.

The twin turbo propellor B200 is a continuation of the King Air line produced by Beechcraft, which began in the 1970s. It is powered by dual Pratt & Whitney Canada PT6A-42 turboprop engines and the standard passenger door has been replaced with a large cargo door to facilitate patient loading and unloading.

The B200 has a standard two pilot installation but, in line with most operators, the RFDS typically operates the aircraft in single pilot mode. The cabin is usually configured with two stretcher beds and three seats with the custom medical modifications and equipment common to all RFDS fixed-wing aircraft.

Global first

The RFDS has four Pilatus PC-24 high-speed jets that have the capacity for three stretchered patients and two medical teams consisting of four doctors and nurses. The service said the PC-24s modified with an aeromedical aircraft were the first of their kind in Australia and globally and can land and take off on unsealed runways as short as 2,625ft.

The jets have a top speed of 490mph, a range of 2,240 miles and a maximum altitude of 45,000ft. They mainly service the vast and thinly populated regions of Western Australia, the Northern Territory and South Australia, where their speed and range make them highly effective for aeromedical services.

The equipment on board likens it to a flying intensive care unit and the PC-24 can use the highways that criss-cross the states as a runway to pick up injured or ill patients when needed. It is a far cry from the incident in 1917 that was the inspiration for establishing the RFDS when it took a doctor one week to travel from Perth to the scene.

EC-145 adventure
The two EC-145 helicopters are operated in a partnership with Fortesque Metals and are typically used for patient retrievals within a 150-mile radius of the Perth base. However, that changed in May 2024 when one of the Airbus helicopters needed to retrieve an injured man from a remote fishing community on the Abrolhos Islands in the Indian Ocean around 274 miles northwest of Perth. The seriously ill man was found slumped over a fishing boat on Big Rat Island and nearby workers used a Quad bike to get him to the local nursing post, where he was cared for overnight by a nurse, supported by a telehealth consultation with an RFDS doctor in Perth.

The airstrip on the island is not long enough to accommodate an RFDS fixed-wing aircraft so the next morning the Airbus EC-145 flew to nearby Geraldton on the mainland to refuel and then on to Big Rat Island. The pilot landed on the island's rocky limestone terrain and the on-board doctor and nurse helped transfer the sick man back to Geraldton Health Campus where he was treated and later released.

In an amazing coincidence, the week before the incident an RFDS team carried out a feasibility mission to Big Rat Island. A team of pilots, a doctor and a logistics specialist assessed the island's airstrip conditions, clinical requirements and options for helicopter flight routes and refuelling, so when the call came the RFDS knew exactly what was required.

A rich aviation history
As it nears its centenary, the RFDS can look back on a rich history of developing aeromedical services in the Australian outback, that started in Queensland in 1928 and

▼ RFDS turboprops are typically flown with one pilot. RFDS

◄ The RFDS has a fleet of 81 aircraft based around Australia. Paul Sadler

▲ RFDS pilots undertake a rigorous training programme. RFDS

▼▶ There are 23 aircraft bases in the RFDS network. RFDS

▼ An aeromedical precinct is being built in Brisbane Airport. Brisbane Airport

within a decade had expanded to include Victoria, Western Australia, South Australia and New South Wales.

The service has operated many aircraft over its 97 years, starting with the Qantas de Havilland DH.50 that was followed by a variety of airplanes including the DH.83 Fox Moth, DH.84 Dragon, DH.104 Dove and the de Havilland Australia DHA-3 Drover.

Between the 1950s and 1970s, the fleet was mainly a mix of Beechcraft, Cessna and Piper aircraft, including the Beechcraft Baron, Travel Air, Queen Air and Duke aircraft. The RFDS also used Cessna 180, 182 and 421 aircraft and Piper Cherokees and Piper PA31 Navajos.

In that period, the New South Wales section operated two British-built Beagle B.206 Mk 2s, until they were replaced in the 1970s with the Australian-made GAF Nomad. Later additions include Cessna 404 and Cessna 441 types as the aeromedical evacuation aircraft settled on the Pilatus PC-12 and Beechcraft King Air 200 series, which are the workhorses today.

A new era

In large Australian cities, emergency helicopters can deliver patients directly to the hospital via a helipad that is usually located within the hospital precinct. Fixed-wing air ambulances such as the RFDS aircraft land at either the main capital city airport or secondary general aviation airports on the fringes of the city.

Brisbane Airport is Australia's fastest-growing and most progressive airport with a relatively new second parallel runway that is in use 24/7, as distinct from

the night curfews at Sydney and Adelaide airports. It is Queensland's capital city airport and a busy destination for aeromedical flights from patients in the far north and west of the state.

In 2024, construction of an aeromedical precinct began at the airport to serve people living in regional, rural and remote communities. The AU$217m (£105m) precinct is being built between the parallel runways and will be home to aircraft and resources for the Royal Flying Doctor Service, LifeFlight, Retrieval Services Queensland and Queensland Police Service Aviation Capability Group.

It will have capacity for 26 aircraft and include aircraft parking and hangar space, along with administrative space for the organisations located at the airport. A new patient transfer facility is being built to care for people transitioning between aircraft and road ambulances, with aircraft having direct access to and from the runways.

In financial year 2024, the RFDS flew 4,611 patients to Brisbane Airport while LifeFlight jets airlifted 528 and its helicopters transported 552 people. On average, 60 patients were aeromedically transported every day throughout Queensland with around 18 of those transferred to and from Brisbane hospitals via Brisbane Airport.

Brisbane Airport has been a principal partner of the Royal Flying Doctor Service Queensland since November 2009. Aeromedical flights are given the highest priority, carrying premature babies to the Mater Hospital, children to the Queensland Children's Hospital and critical patients to hospitals across Brisbane.

▲ **The Pilatus PC-12s are excellent all-rounders for the RFDS.** RFDS

▼ **The EC-145 retrieved a patient from Big Rat Island in the Indian Ocean.** RFDS

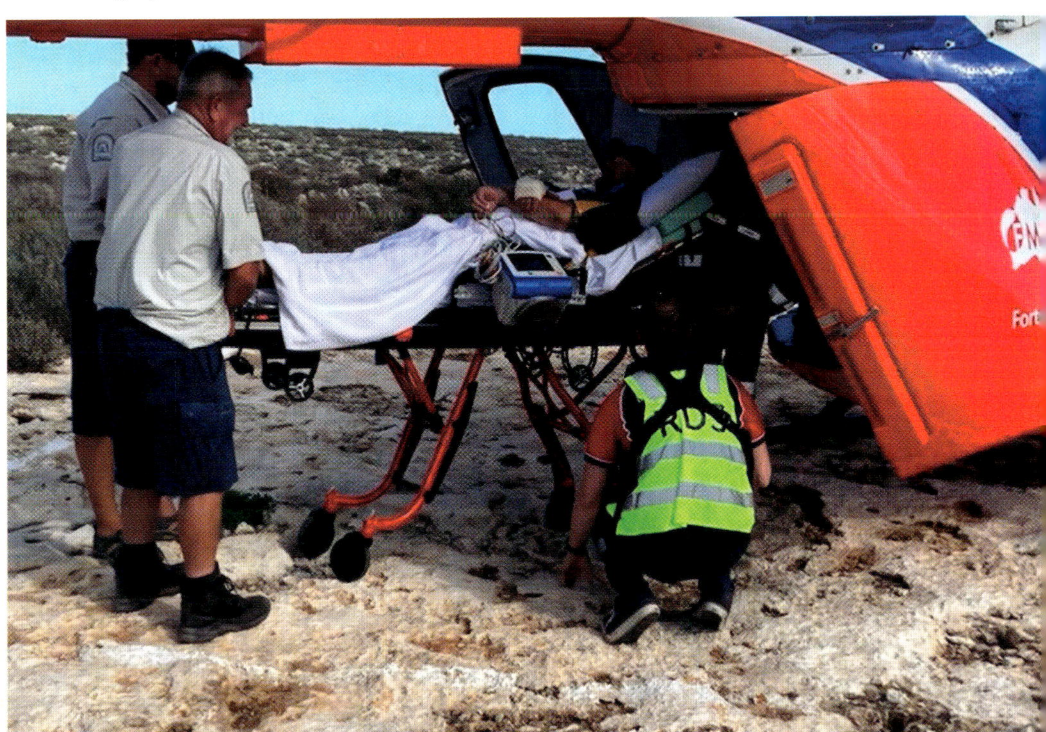

Air Ambulances

Every day aircraft are saving lives by getting medical specialists to ill and injured patients and providing critical life-sustaining care during transit to hospitals.

Police officers, firefighting pilots and air paramedics all talk about the so-called 'golden hour', which is that short but critical time when emergency services need to be with a patient to really make a difference. Medical assistance that takes too long to arrive or doesn't arrive at all can be the difference between life and death, which is why aircraft play such a vital role in emergency medical services.

Using aircraft as air ambulances was a response to the climbing road toll in Germany in the 1960s, when a group of doctors realised that injured patients were dying because medical help was too slow to arrive. In 1967, there were around 20,000 road deaths and experts determined that 15-20% of the injured could have been saved if emergency care had arrived sooner.

In 1970, Germany's automobile club, ADAC, established the first permanent helicopter emergency medical services (HEMS) base in Munich with an MBB Bo 105. Today, there are more than 80 air rescue locations from various operators in Germany and ADAC crews operate over 50 Airbus aircraft, including H145s, H135s and EC135s, from close to 40 stations.

Most major cities are now served by an aeromedical service and have at least one hospital with a helipad that receives aircraft 24/7, particularly in cases where a long journey in a road ambulance is not a viable option. Emergency medical aircraft are fitted to the same standard as hospital emergency rooms, with an array of equipment and systems that can sustain life until more specialist care is available.

Away from emergency cases is the air ambulance segment where fixed-wing aircraft repatriate ill or injured patients to their home nation or transfer those living in rural or remote communities to major metropolitan hospitals for specialist treatment or assessment.

The aircraft manufacturers have played their part by adapting aircraft with bigger doors, flat floors and medical systems or by adding the special mission technology needed. There is a vibrant global industry in designing and configuring bespoke cabins which allows for a large range of aircraft to be modified for aeromedical services.

Swiss Saviours

Swiss Air-Rescue Rega (Rega) is a not-for-profit private foundation that is financed by more than 3.6 million patrons to provide professional

▼ Emergency helicopters are saving lives on a daily basis. OAMTC

medical assistance by air to people in distress around the clock, 365 days a year. Its services are primarily geared towards the needs of the Swiss population whether or not the ensuing costs are covered.

Rega said it utilises the private funding model so it can operate independently in the service of patients and because it takes an active stand against the commercialisation of air rescue. It operates a fleet of fixed-wing and rotary aircraft from 14 bases across Switzerland that are sited to ensure crews can reach any location in the country within 15 minutes flying time.

In 2024, Rega's Operations Centre organised 19,667 missions with 14,714 of those operated by helicopters, 1,367 by jets or scheduled services and 3,586 missions on behalf of the Swiss Alpine Rescue. Helicopter crews performed 2,848 missions after darkness had fallen and, in total, 12,847 patients were transported on board Rega's jets and helicopters.

Rega has a fleet of 20 helicopters operating from its 14 bases, although six are reserve aircraft either in maintenance or needed

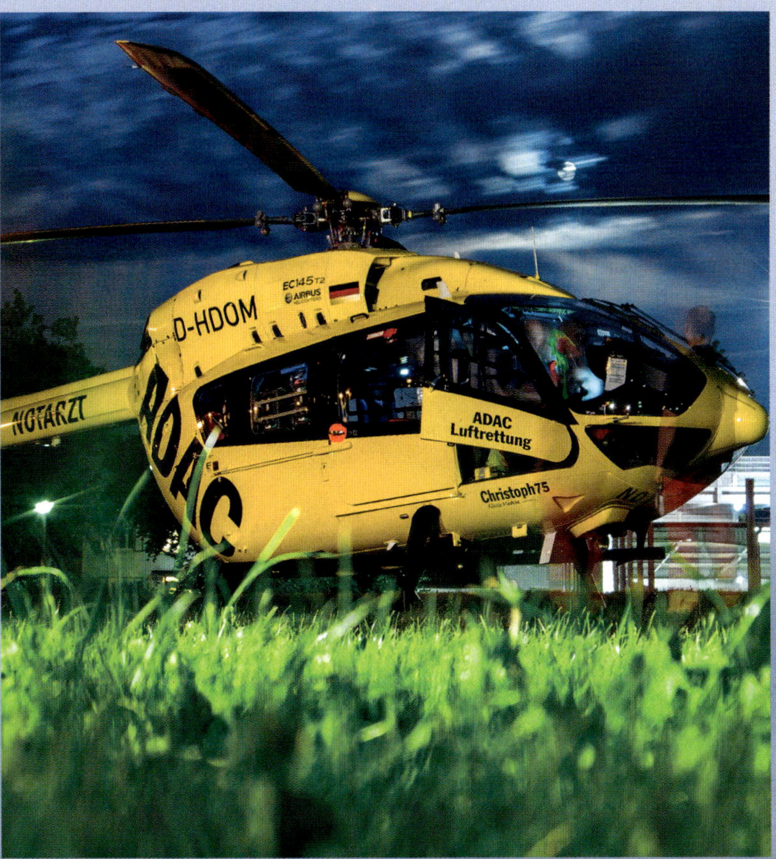

◄ Germany's ADAC established the first HEMS base in 1970. ADAC

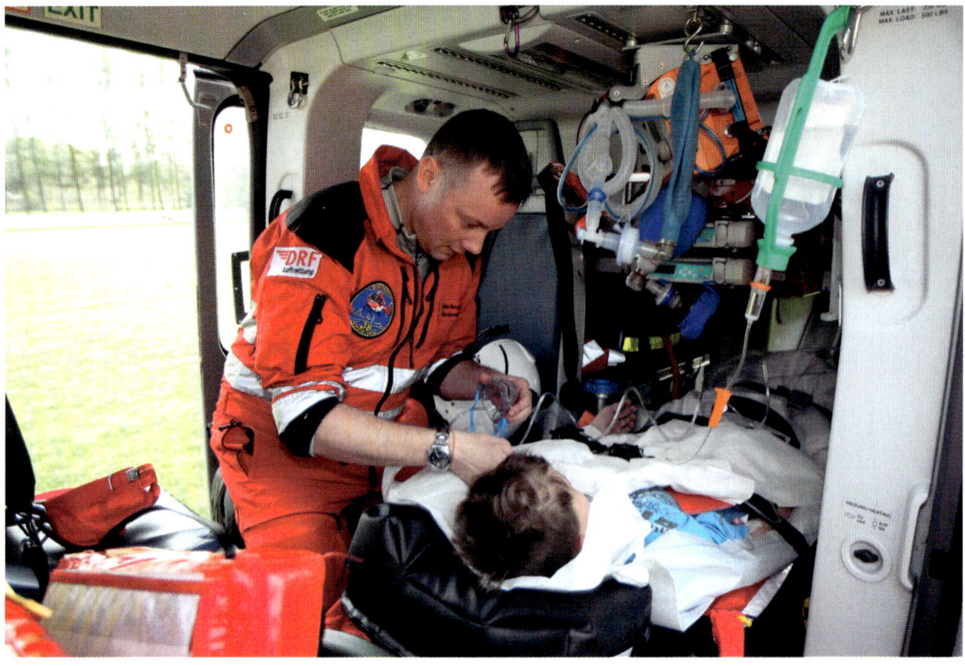

▲ HEMS aircraft are fitted with the latest medical equipment. DRF

▲▶ Increased fatalities in vehicle accidents prompted the birth of HEMS. ARA

▼ Emergency aircraft carry a full range of medical equipment. Airbus

for training. The fleet is in transition, but Rega said it currently contains eight Airbus H145s, one EC135 and 11 AugustaWestland Da Vincis, the last of these a helicopter made to meet Rega's specifications.

The fixed-wing fleet includes three Bombardier Challenger 650 jets that in 2024 operated to 400 different airports and airfields globally for patient repatriation flights. In 2024, these jets spent 4,733 hours in the air, operating 1,033 missions that repatriated 1,029 injured or ill patients.

In December 2022, Rega announced it was embarking on a renewal of its entire helicopter fleet by replacing all the rotary aircraft with the latest five-bladed Airbus H145s. It had purchased a number of H145s earlier that year and was obviously delighted enough with their performance to sign up for nine more.

The H145s will replace the ageing AugustaWestland Da Vinci aircraft that were developed to meet the clearly defined specifications laid out by Rega. These helicopters, which were purchased in 2009, have been stationed at all the mountain bases and operated successfully in terms of flying characteristics, emergency medical equipment and maintenance.

In April 2025, the first five-blade H145 was delivered to its new home at the Lausanne base and the fleet transformation will be completed by the end of 2026. Adding a fifth rotor blade has been a great success for Airbus and the added power increases safety on rescue flights in the challenging and mountainous environment.

A multidisciplinary team comprising physicians, paramedics and engineers spent two years developing the new cabin layout. The spacious interior features sufficient room for the specialised equipment needed for medical interventions, which is particularly important when transferring intensive care patients.

The H145 is able to carry an additional load of 150kg, which allows for more medical equipment and will also be effective when mountain rescuers are onboard and need to use winches in difficult terrain. The capability to perform winch rescues is another reason why the Airbus H145 is an ideal choice for Rega's operations in the Swiss Alps.

Pilots also have significant new features, including a navigation and avionics system specially designed for Rega. The new system will allow even more precise instrument approach procedures, while additional spotlights mean that landing sites in rough terrain can be better illuminated during night missions. Airbus has designed the navigation and avionics system to allow instrument flight procedures to be performed in narrow valleys or challenging terrain even in poor visibility.

The Lausanne base conducts around 800 rescue missions annually, covering interhospital transfers, accidents in the mountains and cases of acute illness.

AIRBUS H140

The launch of any new aircraft is usually full of positive marketing messages but often short on details, but that is not the case with the recent launch of the new Airbus H140 twin-engined helicopter. The multi-mission helicopter was launched in March 2025 at VERTICON in Dallas, Texas. Airbus said the 3-tonne class H145 complements the H135 and H145 and that customers will benefit from

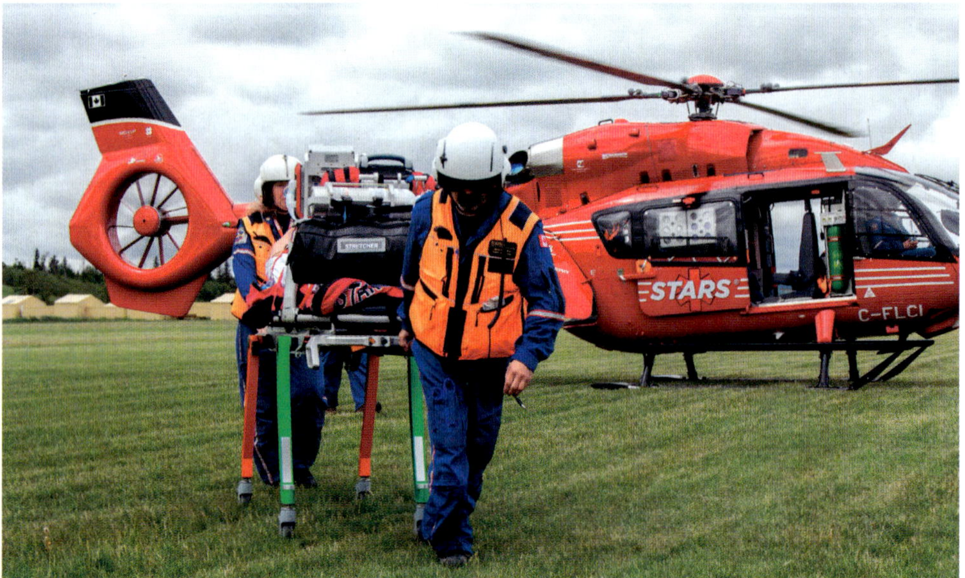

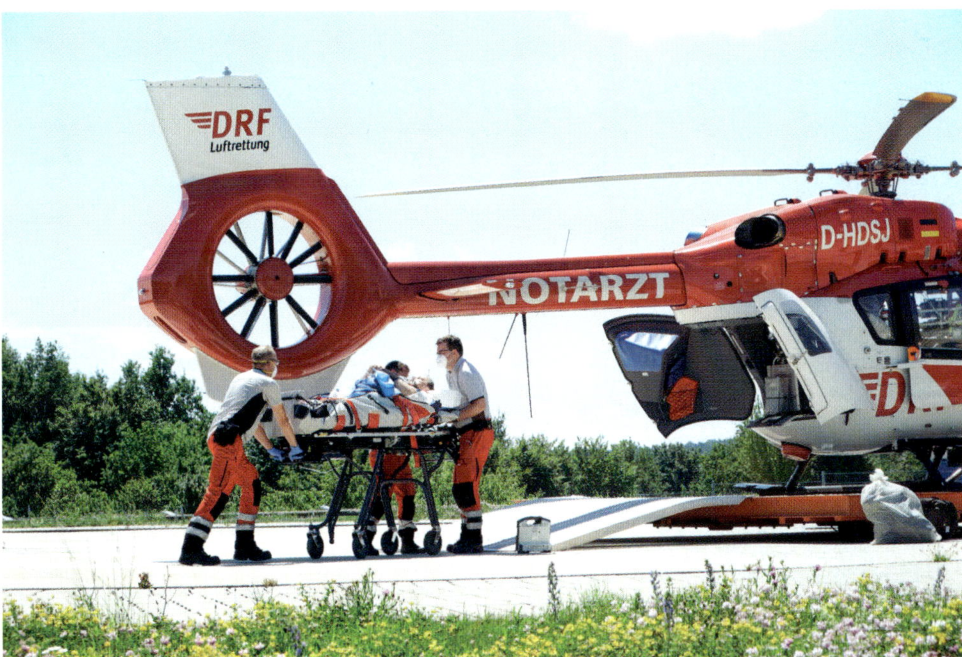

an enlarged cabin that was sized for an optimised engine performance.

An interesting aspect of the launch was that the full-scale model displayed was presented in an emergency medical services configuration. Airbus has been very successful in this market segment with the H135 and H145, and it appears it wants to cement its leadership with a new mid-sized rotorcraft.

The H140 features a T-shaped tail boom with an optimised Fenestron that reduces sound levels, new powerful Safran 2E engines and the widely acclaimed five-blade bearing-less main rotor. The enlarged cabin space allows for larger windows and, depending on the configuration, for up to six people seated comfortably.

To increase accessibility, Airbus designed large clamshell doors and the high tail boom to accommodate the use of different types of stretcher systems, including intensive care stretchers and transport incubators, while the large sliding doors facilitate easy access to the cabin.

The new helicopter will be equipped with the Airbus Helicopters' Helionix avionics systems that is also incorporated in the H135, H145, H160 and H175. When combined with the four-axis autopilot, Helionix offers an innovative cockpit layout to enhance situational awareness, reduce pilot workload and increase safety during missions.

The cabin features a flat floor designed for helicopter emergency medical services that gives operators the flexibility and modularity to configure the cabin to suit their missions. The stretchers can be on the left or the right side of the cabin or on each side and the H140 will have specific HEMS lighting in the cabin and for loading.

Customer interest

It is common practice for aircraft manufacturers to bank orders and announce them at a major event such as VERTICON, the Paris Air Show or others held in the UK, Dubai and Singapore.

Airbus confirmed that the emergency medical services H140 is not expected to enter service until 2028, but given the state of global supply chains it is anyone's guess as to when the aircraft will actually be certified and available for operations.

The Airbus optimism for a 2028 entry into service means there has been no shortage of operators lining up to sign an agreement, letter of intent or place an order for the H140. At VERTICON 2025, Airbus announced that seven operators had made commitments for up to 74 H140s, with four customers based in the US and three in Europe. These customers include Air Methods, Global Medical Response, Stat MedEvac, Metro Aviation, DRF Luftrettung, OAMTC and ADAC Luftrettung. All are existing Airbus operators, with Air Methods being the largest civil operator of Airbus helicopters worldwide, with a fleet that includes H125s, H130s, H135s and H145s.

Flight testing of the H140 began in 2023 and one prototype has already flown above 145kt in horizontal flight. Airbus said it will be developing four dedicated prototypes, with a second to be added in 2025 and two more in 2026.

Global Medical Response

Global Medical Response (GMR) is a world leader in the air medical industry, operating from 380 base locations under brands including AirMed International, Guardian Flight,

▲ The larger cabins of the H145 are attractive for HEMS operators. Airbus

▼ Swiss Air-Rescue Riga operates from 14 bases across Switzerland. Rega

▲ Airbus has launched its H140 with orders from major HEMS operators. Airbus

▼ Rega's fleet of AW109 Da Vincis are currently being replaced by H145s. Rega

REACH Air Medical Services, Air Evac Lifeteam and Med-Trans Corporation. It has a fleet of around 486 aircraft that includes 383 rotorary and 103 fixed-wing aircraft, with nearly 200 Airbus helicopters in the fleet or on order. It is the leading provider of air ambulance services in the US, with missions including medical evacuations, critical care transports and long-haul repatriation services.

Helicopters crewed by a pilot, a flight nurse and a paramedic are on duty seven days a week to respond to medical emergencies or to transport patients between medical facilities. Modern fixed-wing aircraft are manned by fully trained and experienced staff to transport patients in remote and rural locations to large metropolitan hospitals.

AirMed International delivers long-haul repatriation services using a fleet of fully customised and permanent medically configured jets supported by GMR's despatch, flight and medical teams. Emergency air operations are provided by Air Evac Lifeteam, Guardian Flight, Med-Trans and REACH.

The REACH helicopter fleet includes the twin-engined IFR-capable H135, as well as the single-engined H125 (also known as the AStar AS350) and H130. These have a cruise speed of approximately 120-160mph and the fleet also includes single-engined VFR-only Bell 407 aircraft.

On the fixed-wing side, REACH operates King Air B200 twin-engined IFR-capable pressurised aircraft and the single-engined Pilatus PC-12 that can carry two patients and attendant

medical crew. It has a top speed of 310mph and a range of 900 miles round trip, while the Pilatus PC-12 has a maximum speed of 300mph and a range of about 2,500 miles.

REACH is at the forefront of private emergency service operators and was only the fifth programme in the US to fully implement night-vision goggles (NVG). It has operated missions utilising NVG technology since February 2004 and was the first air ambulance company to receive FAA approval to respond off airway, using its own GPS routes to specific hospitals.

Beechcraft King Air

Across the spectrum of emergency air operations, Beechcraft King Air turboprops can be found in almost all segments, including aerial law enforcement, search and rescue, border protection and emergency medical services. King Air B200 and B360 aircraft are particularly popular for emergency medical and patient transport missions in all weather and environments, including the outback of Australia, the heat of Greece or the colder climates of northern Europe.

In May 2025, Textron Aviation, the owner of brands including Beechcraft, Cessna, Hawker and Bell, announced the delivery of a Beechcraft King Air 360C to Greece's Ministry of Health and National Center for Emergency Care (EKAV). The aircraft acquisition is part of a global health initiative that has funded five aircraft, including two King Air 350Cs and the new 360C. The specially configured

aircraft feature a cargo door and air-medical system to ensure patients in remote areas can be transported to central locations in Greece and Europe. All three King Airs will be operated out of Elefsis Airbase in Greece to strengthen the nation's air ambulance services.

The air ambulance conversion was completed by Fargo Jet Center at its special mission aircraft modification facility at Hector International Airport in Fargo, North Dakota. Fargo Jet Center is a specialist in converting aircraft for special missions and has completed numerous air ambulance conversions on aircraft including King Airs, Pilatus PC-12s, Learjets, Cessna Caravans and Citations.

To meet the diverse needs of its customers, Fargo Jet Center provides a full custom air medical design and installation solution to match those needs and missions. A typical configuration would be fitted with a 52in cargo door and heavyweight landing gear, a Proline 21 integrated Max-Viz enhanced

vision system and interior/exterior LED lighting. The interior is equipped with the latest medical equipment that transforms the cabin into an airborne emergency department. It will have room for one patient

and up to six medical personnel, with an intercom system that has multiple isolation configurations to allow the flight crew and air medical team to communicate with ground-based EMS and hospital staff while simultaneously making Iridium phone calls inflight.

The aircraft also features digital pressurisation that automatically schedules cabin pressure on both climb and descent, which is important when transporting ill or injured patients. The King Air 360 has a maximum range of 1,806nm, a cruise speed of 321kts and a useful load of 5,145lb. It can carry 11 occupants and take off from a runway length of 3,300ft.

Leonardo HEMS

Italian aerospace manufacturer Leonardo has been a major player in HEMS for decades and today its AW139 and AW169 helicopters are a common sight on the helipads of major hospitals worldwide. The same

▲ Beechcraft King Airs play a significant role in emergency transfers. J Alan Paul

◄ Special mission equipment and modified cabins are fitted to all HEMS aircraft. Airbus

▼ The extra power and stability of the H145 suit mountain operations. Airbus

▲ **More than 50 AW139s are used on HEMS missions in Australia.** Leonardo

Leonardo aircraft types also have a strong presence in search and rescue missions and the multi-role nature of the platforms means they can work in tandem or combine missions between the two sectors.

The light intermediate twin-engined AW169 is especially suited to HEMS operations where its power, range and regular-shaped cabin stand out from the competition. In a typical HEMS layout the AW169 can accommodate up to two patients, five medical personnel and a full suite of critical medical equipment, with the room for easy access to patients. It also has an APU-mode that enables the cabin to remain powered with rotors stopped, which allows the medical to control the cabin environment and lighting, as well as keeping vital equipment operating.

Since the AW139 was certified in 2004, Leonardo has gained orders for more than 1,500 aircraft from more than 300 customers in around 90 countries. The AW139s feature advanced navigation and collision avoidance systems to enhance situational awareness and reduce pilots' workload in often stressful and challenging environments.

Leonardo has established a significant presence in the Australian emergency services market with their AW139s and AW169s operating on missions including aerial law enforcement, search and rescue and emergency medical flights. More than 75 AW139s are used by Australian operators, around 50 of them for emergency medical operations.

For nearly 50 years, the not-for-profit organisation LifeFlight has delivered emergency and critical care and today operates from nine bases across Australia and in Singapore. Its fleet includes four Bombardier Challenger 604 jets and AW139, Bell 412 and BK117 helicopters. In March 2025, LifeFlight and its joint venture partner StarFlight celebrated ten years of operating AW139s by ordering four additional aircraft, with deliveries expected to be completed in 2027. The latest orders means that the combined AW139 fleet of LifeFlight and StarFlight will be one of the largest in Australia.

▶ **AW139s have gained a strong presence in Australian HEMS.** Michael Doran

▼ **Emergency aircraft and medical crews operate in all regions.** Airbus

691/25

Eyes in the Sky

▲ Bell believes one airborne officer can do the work of up to nine on the ground.
Bell

While not many people buy an aircraft in their lifetime, many buy a car. After talking to the experts, there seems little difference between aircraft and road vehicles when it comes to making the right decision.

Where aircraft are concerned, the first question should not be which one is the best, but rather what do you want to do with it – once that is clear the choice becomes obvious; the needs of a police agency in London are very different from those in Anchorage, Hong Kong, Geneva or Mexico City, which is why there are so many aircraft types used in policing.

The reality is that there are no law enforcement aircraft, but there are hundreds of everyday fixed-wing and rotary aircraft that have been fitted out with specialist equipment to perform that role. It makes far more sense to view the aircraft as an airborne platform with an appropriate sized cabin that operators equip with the mission equipment suited to their needs.

In 1948, Bell helicopter delivered the world's first helicopter to be manufactured and put into police service when it handed over a Bell 47D to the New York City Police Department. The sight of a police helicopter is now common in most large cities and they are an essential tool in keeping communities and law enforcement officers safe.

A Bell Helicopter report cited a study that estimated an officer in a helicopter could potentially do the work of up to nine officers on the ground and that from a helicopter an officer can see 30 times more than they can on the ground. The crew in the air can see every side of a building, the roof and behind fences or around corners, but the officer on the ground might only see two sides of the building.

This is a true force-multiplier effect and a major benefit that aircraft bring to law enforcement, particularly as the US Department of Justice reported that 93% of police aircraft conduct routine patrols and 98% are used for direct surveillance. Police aircraft have proven their worth since 1948 because they save lives, protect citizens and allow forces to react to events more quickly.

Rotary responders

Airbus, Bell, Leonardo, Sikorsky and Robinson all have a visible presence in the law enforcement sector, ranging for light to heavy helicopters used on missions including surveillance, tactical operations, transport of strike teams, real-time intelligence gathering, pursuits and patrol activities.

◄ Los Angeles PD operates the Airbus H125 on police support, covert ops and pursuits. Airbus

▼ The modern Airbus H160 is increasingly used for law enforcement missions. Airbus

Airbus

Airbus began its involvement in aerial law enforcement (ALE) in the 1960s when the French Gendarmerie Nationale introduced Alouette II helicopters. It is a leader in the field and has a full range of aircraft flying ALE missions, including single-engined H125 and twin-engined H135 and H145 variants operating globally.

The H125 is a popular choice in North and Latin America while light twin engine aircraft like the H135 are more prevalent in Europe due to stringent safety regulations. The UK's National Police Air Service has a fleet of 20 helicopters that includes 16 Airbus H135s and four of the larger H145s, with an order for a further seven H135s in place.

The Los Angeles Police Department operates the smaller H125 aircraft on missions such as high-speed

vehicle pursuits, providing support for undercover operations and general assistance to ground-based enforcement officers. In very different conditions US Customs and Border Protection fly the H125 along the southwestern US border countering threats from alien smuggling, drug trafficking and terrorism.

Airbus understands the importance of an integrated cabin and offers a mission management system that provides crew with tactical elements of connectivity as well as sensors on the operator workstation.

◄ Twin-engined Airbus H135 aircraft meet European safety requirements. Airbus

▲ **The lighter single-engined H125s are a popular choice in the US.** Airbus

▼ **USA's Fort Worth Police Department added a second Bell 505 in 2024.** Bell

The mission management system is natively integrated into the aircraft and centralises all the sensors, which makes it possible to retransmit and receive all the necessary information for the mission. The ALE mission equipment also includes loud speakers, an electro optical system, moving maps, data downlink, hoist, rappelling bar and a searchlight.

The H125 has a maximum range of 335nm, a fast cruise speed of 133kts and maximum endurance of 4hrs 20mins, while the comparable numbers for the twin engine H135 are 449nm, 136kts and 4hrs 46mins.

The H145 can carry up to two pilots and ten passengers and the H160 has room for two pilots and 12 passengers, meaning they are both effective choices for inserting SWAT or fast-response teams either by rappelling or landing. For multi-role agencies these two are also well suited for search and rescue, emergency medical and counter-terrorism operations.

The H145 has a range of 439nm, a fast cruise speed of 130kts and 4hrs 31mins endurance compared with the H160's range of 442nm, fast cruise of 144kts and endurance of 4hrs 12mins. Japan's National Police Agency became the first parapublic operator of the H160 when it added one aircraft in December 2024 and another in January 2025.

In March 2025, the New York State Police became the first law enforcement agency in the US to add the H160 when it ordered one H160 and three H145s, adding to a 2024 order for two H145s. The New York State Police Aviation Unit was formed in 1931 and supports police and lifesaving and environmental conservation agencies across the state.

The relatively new twin-engine H160 is frequently used for parapublic missions including law enforcement, search and rescue, emergency medical services and offshore transportation. It is currently in service in countries including Brazil, Canada, France, Japan, Malaysia, Philippines, Saudi Arabia, the United Kingdom and the United States.

Bell

Bell helicopters are used by law enforcement agencies in more than 120 countries, including around 300 police operators in the US. Its customers range in size from single aircraft, single pilot operations to those with more than 20 aircraft

multiple Cessna 208B Grand Caravan EX airplanes.

PolAir responds to more than 7,000 formal requests and conducts more than 20,000 patrols annually. The multi-role agency conducts tactical operations, patrols, crime response support, including pursuits, traffic incidents and offender searches, as well as search and rescue missions.

The 429s contain all of the usual ALE equipment, including FLIR (forward looking infrared) camera, high definition video camera, data downlink, tactical radio, mapping, searchlight, rescue hoist and touch screen digital cockpit with a GPS navigation system.

In March 2025, the Queensland Police Force announced it had entered into a contract for three Bell 429s, doubling its existing fleet of three 429s. The aircraft will be fitted with night-vision capabilities and cameras

▼ **Multi-role Bell 429s are used by law enforcement agencies worldwide.** Bell

and 150 personnel in a dedicated police aviation unit.

Many types of Bell helicopters are used by law enforcement agencies and while all have a role the most popular choices are the Bell 429, 505 and Subaru Bell 412EPX. Bell said around 25% of 429s sold globally are used in public safety yet public safety is not 25% of the helicopter industry.

The multi-mission capability of the 429 makes it the popular choice as it is equally effective on patrol right through to heavy rescue missions. It is an advanced single pilot, seven passenger aircraft that is certified for single or dual-pilot instrument flight rules operations.

The 429 has a spacious cabin volume with an agile interior and a flat floor that can be effortlessly converted from passenger to cargo operations in minutes. It has a maximum cruise of 150kts, a range of 411nm and a maximum endurance of 4hrs 30mins. The 429 is widely used in Australia by law enforcement and other public service operators, such as the New South Wales (NSW) Police Aviation Command, known locally as PolAir.

The NSW police force covers 500,000m², which is an area three times the size of California and twice the size of Texas. To do that it utilises a fleet of three patrol-equipped Bell 429s, two SAR-configured 412EPIs, several unmanned aircraft and

◄ **Bell 505s are fitted with modern glass cockpits with twin LCD screens.** Omaha PD

▼ **Airbus H145s are favoured by police forces for their speed and endurance.** Airbus

to assist officers in tracking vehicles, apprehending offenders and locating missing persons from the air.

In late 2024, Bell announced the sale of a second 505 to the Fort Worth Police Department in the US state of Texas. Since its inception, the police department has used a series of Bell aircraft to advance their public safety aerial capabilities including Bell 47s and 206 Jet Rangers.

The first Bell 505 was delivered in 2021 during a ceremony that commemorated the 70-year relationship between Bell and the department. The second 505 will be used to increase public safety and search and rescue missions. The 505 has a maximum cruise speed of 125kts, a range of 306nm, endurance of around four hours and a service ceiling of 18,610ft.

Leonardo

For nearly 70 years, Italian aerospace company Leonardo has been supporting law enforcement agencies and today there are more than 700 of its helicopters operating ALE missions with 120 operators in almost 50 countries. It has five new-generation aircraft in the sector starting with the single-engine AW119X and the light twin-engine AW109 Trekker.

Airbus has been successful in the commercial aircraft market by offering a family of jets that grow in line with their customers' growth and Leonardo has followed a similar approach with its AW139, AW169 and AW189 family. These three share the same design approach and are designed to be inherently multi-role, which fits well with ALE missions.

The AW139 and AW169 platforms are highly versatile and customisable for various law enforcement missions, including surveillance, search and rescue, tactical operations, passenger transport and disaster relief.

These two are well suited for public safety missions as they meet the FAA Part 29 certification standards with a full crashworthy airframe and seats, wide emergency exits, engine burst containment, 30+ minutes

▶ Leonardo's family of AW169 and AW139 are part of Italy's ALE force. Leonardo

▶ This AW139 is used by Australia's VicPol for tactical missions. Michael Doran

▼ Omaha Police Department is another US agency operating the Bell 505. Omaha PD

dry-run main gearbox and one engine inoperative capability in all phases of flight.

An important feature for multi-role operations is being able to quickly reconfigure the aircraft from one mission to the next, such as going from law enforcement tracking flights to transporting injured people to a hospital. The AW139 and AW169 have large cabin volumes with a flat ceiling and floor that facilitates quick changes to the cabin layout.

The AW169 has a specialised missions console and can carry up to ten passengers or be configured to hold two stretchers. It has wide 1.6m (63in) doors that facilitate fast-roping, rappelling and hoisting operations that provide tactical diversity and enhance response options. It can accommodate up to ten passengers and has a maximum cruise speed of 144kts, whereas the AW139 can fly at 165kts at a maximum range of 641nm.

The larger AW139 is the best-selling twin-engine helicopter in its class with more than 1,000 customers worldwide. It also features the largest cabin in its class that can seat up to 15 passengers or ten deployable law enforcement officers with the same reconfiguration advantages as the AW169.

Its integrated avionics system provides operators with the maximum benefit from the sensors and communications equipment required for ALE missions, while its power reserve provides Category A Class 1 performance to operate safely in a wide range of conditions.

AW139s are used across the spectrum of parapublic and security missions and in Australia they are used by police, search and rescue, offshore transport and emergency medical operators. VicPol, the aviation arm of Victoria Police, renewed its fleet with three AW139s replacing ageing Dauphin AS365 helicopters in the early 2020s.

A surprising outcome was that crew fatigue reduced significantly, which was attributed to the larger cabin, improved ergonomics and an overall healthier cabin environment. Encountering less fatigue allowed crews to feel more comfortable and fly for longer, which is important on emergency missions as their territory is about the same size as the UK.

Fixed-wing ALE

Law enforcement agencies around the world use a variety of fixed-wing aircraft for surveillance, reconnaissance, interdiction and transport missions. The advantages

▼◀ **In Australia, NSW PolAir renewed its fleet with Bell 429s.** Bell

▼ **Polk County Sheriff in the US uses Robinson R66 aircraft.** Robinson

they offer over helicopters are longer range, faster speed and more endurance, which means they can patrol for hours without needing to return for fuel.

In the world of policing, airplanes and helicopters support each other and combine to expand the reach and efficiency of law enforcement and public safety agencies, as will unmanned aircraft in the not too distant future.

In the US, agencies such as the FBI, DEA, Customs and Border Protection (CBP), state and local police use fixed-wing aircraft equipped with the same type of special mission equipment as fitted on ALE helicopters.

Some of the popular aircraft types used by law enforcement in the US include the Cessna 182, Cessna 206, Beechcraft King Air and Pilatus PC-12, many of which appear on other pages in this publication. In the UK, the National Police Air Service operates the Italian Vulcanair P68R for surveillance of large public events, longer-range searches and crowd support operations.

In Australia, aircraft such as the Beechcraft Super King Air and Cessna 208 are part of public safety fleets where their extended range is needed when operating in outback and rural areas well away from capital city hubs.

Modern light twins such as the Tecnam P2006T and the Diamond DA42 MPP are used in Europe for border patrols, public order, large events, maritime surveillance and environmental monitoring.

Other airplanes that operate law enforcement operations include

Piper PA-31 Navajo and Piper PA-34 Seneca, Aero Commander and Twin Commander, Cessna 206 Stationair and Beechcraft 200/350 series turboprops.

Finding targets

While rotary and fixed-wing law enforcement aircraft carry a cabin full of specialised mission equipment, the one technology that links them all is the camera transmitting those all-important images. It was many decades ago when TV news bulletins started featuring images and live feeds and today that technology is the central element of ALE missions.

Public safety operators rely on images from electro-optical infrared (EO/IR) systems to identify targets such as vehicles, offenders, missing persons or a life-raft bobbing in a raging ocean. The startling thing is that EO/IR systems can find the target long before the aircraft gets

to the scene, with car number plates readable from a mile away.

Teledyne FLIR

It must be the ultimate accolade in marketing when the name of a product turns into the generic name for all other products doing the same function, but that is what Teledyne FLIR has achieved. Teledyne is one of the world's leading makers of vision-enhancing systems used in defence, public safety, commercial and government markets.

It is common to see Teledyne's FLIR (forward looking infrared) mounted on a gimbal underneath the nose of fixed-wing and rotary aircraft engaged in law enforcement, border protection, firefighting, search and rescue and wildlife protection operations. Teledyne has the widest array of sensors, which are the heart of the system and determine what data is captured.

◄ **Beechcraft King Airs are one of the many aircraft used in law enforcement.** Textron Aviation

The Star SAFIRE 380X is popular in law enforcement because of its capability for HD IR, HD Colour EO, Zoom LLTV, Short wave IR, Laser Rangefinder, Ponter and Illuminator, Laser Designator and HD Video outputs. It also has an integrated moving target indicator (MTI) and de-scintillation filter that removes atmospheric effects to reveal clearer, sharper detail from greater distances.

A good example of scintillation is to think of a long straight road with a heat haze coming off the surface, an effect that obscures images. The 380X has software that cuts through that and extends the range of the camera even further, extending the detection, recognition and identification capabilities of the system.

The system uses multi-tile management to allow the operator to view multiple video sources simultaneously, including all discrete camera payloads plus external video input. With the majority of ALE missions associated with searches, the FLIR system is a critical tool when operators are trying to find the target in a large area – the system can pinpoint the location and reduce the operator's workload.

The MTI helps identify targets earlier and captures images so clearly that it is used by police in future prosecutions, such as those where drugs or weapons are thrown from a moving vehicle. Another strength of the FLIR system is that existing third-party systems, such as a mapping system, can be integrated so the two systems work seamlessly together.

◄ **The FLIR SAFIRE380X is mounted on a gimbal to give operators a clear view.** Teledyne FLIR

▼ **Teledyne FLIR cameras are vital to today's police forces.** Teledyne FLIR

The UK Way

With a fleet of helicopters and fixed-wing aircraft, the UK's National Police Air Service is supporting local police forces throughout England and Wales.

In the United Kingdom, the National Police Air Service (NPAS) has been providing air support to all police forces in England and Wales since 2012. It was formed following a national review of air support by the UK Home Office, and territorial police forces in England and Wales and British Transport Police contribute funding to the air service.

From its headquarters in West Yorkshire, the NPAS Operations Centre is open 24/7 and manages requests for air support from police forces and other agencies across England and Wales. The service has a fleet of 20 helicopters and four fixed-wing aircraft operating from 15 regional bases and in March 2025 the average time to reach the scene of a Priority One incident was 12 minutes and 43 seconds.

The rotary-wing fleet is an all Airbus affair comprising 16 H135 and four H145 helicopters; NPAS also operates four Vulcanair P68R twin-engine aeroplanes. In March 2025, NPAS announced it will be receiving seven new Airbus H135 helicopters with the first due to arrive in 2027.

The service carries out a variety of tasks supporting police forces, including searching for high-risk missing or injured people, searching for suspects, managing vehicle pursuits from the air and assisting with counter-terrorism and specialist firearms operations.

In 2023/2024, the fleet flew a total of 11,619 hours on behalf of police forces and a further 1,373 hours on training, transit and maintenance flights with aircraft deployed 19,690 times.

Finding people

In the year to March 2025, NPAS aircraft located 1,376 vulnerable and missing people, 4,224 crime suspects and 1,987 target vehicles. NPAS head of flight operations Captain Paul Watts said the vast majority of missions are for searches

▼ The NPAS has a fleet of 16 Airbus H135s. NPAS

for missing persons and suspects for all sorts of crimes: "It tends to be vulnerable people who perhaps have mental health problems and have indicated they are going to self-harm, runaway children or elderly people who have gone missing. We go out into the hills and mountains as well as urban areas and that's where we overlap with search and rescue aircraft."

He said that while most work comes from reacting to calls for assistance from local police forces, NPAS also provides proactive missions in support of local crime initiatives, often involving the Vulcanair P68R aircraft: "In the last couple of weeks our fixed-wing aircraft have been assisting a police force in the Midlands which has a problem with off-road bikes and quad bikes," he explained. "We've been actively patrolling and then identifying anti-social behaviour on these vehicles, which quite often also turn out to be stolen."

The NPAS Operations Centre handles more than 100 calls daily, where staff prioritise simultaneous requests for air support when there is a threat-to-life situation. Staff track the aircraft whenever they are airborne and individually monitor six radio channels, which cover England and Wales, plus telephone lines and computer systems digitally linked to local forces.

As well as communicating with police forces, the staff are frequently liaising with search and rescue teams plus officers from prisons, military bases, nuclear power stations and other key national organisations and service providers. The flight duty officer is updated

▲ The helicopter fleet contains both H135 and H145 aircraft. NPAS

▲ **Four NPAS H145s are operated in London.** NPAS

on safety issues, aircraft location, weather conditions, engineering requirements and crew and aircraft availability.

How it works

The helicopters have a crew of three, including the pilot and two tactical flight officers (TFOs), with one of those sitting in the front seat to the left of the pilot and operating the camera system. The rear TFO is the mission controller who operates a suite of mission equipment, including displays of moving maps, camera output and multiple radios.

In a search operation the rear TFO will input the last known location into the mission system, which has software that can calculate likely search areas. While en route, the TFO will be identifying possible search areas and relaying navigation information through to the pilot and camera operator.

"We can slave the camera onto the target quite a long way out so we can actually start the search before getting to the location and then establish a search pattern when we arrive," Capt Watts added. "Open streets are quick to search and you can clear big open fields from far off with a camera sweep, but in undergrowth or wooded areas you need to do a slow and detailed search."

At night, the primary search tool is the thermal camera particularly where there are fewer people and heat sources in the area. The crews can also use night-vision goggles to enhance the scene, but Watts said a lot of the pick-ups are achieved by just looking out of the window or, as he terms it, in the 'old-school way'.

He said: "The human brain is very good at picking up patterns and crews get very experienced at picking out the person who's actively evading the aircraft because they'll behave in a way that actually makes them stand out from the people around them. It's almost like a sixth sense but it's more learned behaviour from years of experience."

The aircraft are fitted with a high-powered searchlight, but nowadays these are not used frequently, although they are useful to guide ground police to a location. The fact is that new-generation thermal cameras are so effective they can pick up whether a subject is wearing shorts or a dress or a hooded jacket and at night the technology is at its best.

▶ **The fleet is located across 15 regional bases.** NPAS

The moving digital maps with a street overlay are another effective policing tool as they allow the TFO to pass on exact location details to ground officers, including surrounding street names for officers heading to the scene. As most of us have seen on TV, the system comes into its own in vehicle pursuits and the quality of the recorded footage produces irrefutable evidence in subsequent trials.

"Everything's recorded, so if the TFO sees something thrown out of a window they will mark it on the map and later rewind to pinpoint the exact location so police can recover discarded clothing, drugs or weapons," he said. "You've got consistency of evidence and can demonstrate exactly where the person has been and what they have done, so it's fantastic evidence in court."

All Airbus fleet

It is a little surprising that the NPAS fleet consists of just Airbus helicopters, but with an order for seven new aircraft placed in early 2025 it's clear the service believes strongly in the brand. Originally, some of the police forces had their own aircraft and when NPAS was established those aircraft were transferred to become the NPAS fleet.

Airbus was successful in winning the new order for seven H135 helicopters after beating off spirited competition from other OEMs in an open process that went on for two years. Watts said the H135 is a great aircraft for what NPAS does and because not a lot of people are transported there is no need for larger helicopters: "The H145s were purchased by the MET Police with an eye on the 2012 London Olympics to meet a requirement to be able to carry a team of armed officers that could be fast-roped into a venue," he said. "They had the ability to deploy them straight into the Olympic Park if necessary and all the H145s are still deployed in London."

The larger H145s differ from the rest of the fleet in that they are equipped with the fleet's most capable camera system, the WESCAM MX-15, which allows the aircraft to operate at higher altitude than the H135s fitted with WESCAM MX-10 systems. This is particularly useful around London with its mix of tall cranes and high-rise buildings.

The ageing H145s are earmarked for replacement by the latest H135s fitted with state-of-the-art WESCAM MX-15 camera systems designed for medium altitude, covert intelligence, surveillance and security operations. The MX-15 supports up to seven payload items including HD thermal, HD daylight, HD low-light and HD SWIR (short-wave infrared) cameras.

Supply chain issues

The NPAS fleet, which includes the most intensively used police helicopters in the world, is maintained by Airbus UK, which has not been immune to global supply chain disruptions. Watts said if maintenance capacity and parts are available, keeping the aircraft in the air is not a major issue, but the specialist mission equipment can be more of a challenge: "Some of that equipment is not unique, but it's not that common and as various

▲ The NPAS has four Italian Vulcanair P68R aircraft. NPAS

◀ Aircraft arrive at high-priority calls in under 13 minutes. NPAS

parts of it become obsolete we have difficulty in replacing them. The airframes themselves need increasing amounts of maintenance, which increases costs and downtime so keeping those airframes airborne is a massive challenge for the MRO and for us operationally."

More than 1,560 twin-engine H135s have been delivered to around 325 operators in 63 countries and by 2024, H135s had clocked up more than 7.5 million flying hours. It is a favourite among law enforcement agencies where it is prized for its speed, range, capacity and lower maintenance costs.

The H135 has a maximum range of 342nm or 449nm if fitted with an external fuel tank, can cruise at 136kts, has a hover ceiling of 7,200ft and endurance of 3hrs 36mins with a standard fuel tank or 4hrs 46mins with the external fuel tank.

It can be fitted with the full gamut of police mission equipment including tactical radios, moving maps, searchlight, mission control console, downlink system, rappelling installation, hoist, night-vision, weather and search radar, wire strike protection and camera technology.

The contract for the seven new H135s has been finalised and after they have been produced at Airbus Helicopters in Germany they will arrive in the UK as bare, green aircraft. Watts said the contract is for complete role-equipped aircraft so they will be joining the NPAS fleet fully kitted-out and ready to go, starting in 2027.

▶ **H145s operated at the 2012 London Olympic Games.**
NPAS

▼ **East Midlands Airport is the base for the Vulcanairs.**
NPAS

Vulcanair P68R

Fixed-wing aircraft play a different, but equally important role in aerial law enforcement and with four twin-engine turboprops, NPAS has significant resource capability at its disposal. It has the Italian Vulcanair P68R, formerly manufactured as the Partenavia P.68 that made its first flight in 1970 and gained certification in 1971, and which was transferred to Vulcanair in 1998.

The four aircraft are based centrally in the UK at East Midlands Airport from where they are despatched to all parts of England and Wales. The twin-engine P68R has six seats, a cruise speed of 168kts, a range of 890nm and with four people on board can stay in the air for nearly six hours.

Watts said the main advantage that fixed-wing aircraft have is their endurance, which means they can cover a long event, such as public demonstrations, sports and other activities where surveillance is required: "Helicopters can do it, but you are constantly rotating aircraft whereas with the fixed-wing we can set up a search pattern for hours on end. It's the same for covering large search areas where it is faster than a helicopter and we can fly it anywhere in the country, operate for two to three hours and return to its base."

The Vulcanairs were fitted with policing and other mission equipment by Austrian company Airborne Technologies, including an integrated radio suite, carbon fibre tactical operator workstation,

◀ National Police Air Service helicopters are operated by one pilot. NPAS

gimbal, embedded stills camera and a touchscreen mission management system.

Fixed-wing impact

An excellent example of a fixed-wing mission is when the NPAS team was enlisted to work with Merseyside Police in planning for the 175th Grand National festival at Aintree racecourse, Merseyside, in the UK.

Over the three days of the festival, the Vulcanair P68R spent 19 hours in the air providing aerial overviews in the before, during and after phases of the public safety operation. Public protests had been planned to disrupt the event that authorities believed would risk the safety of attendees.

On the day of the big race, the aircraft spent more than five hours flying over the course and surrounding roads, neighbourhoods and scrubland, identifying potential pockets of anti-social behaviour.

While patrolling, the crew picked up a diversionary incident of more than 60 protesters trying to scale a perimeter fence and glue themselves to railings. Using the on-board equipment the crew provided vital downlink images to incident commanders for action.

This intelligence combined with real-time images enabled the commander to direct resources to the scene and led to multiple arrests. The airborne surveillance assured the organisers and police commanders that all potential areas of risk were clear of any threat to the public, event personnel, jockeys and horses.

The extended endurance of the Vulcanair allowed it to remain on station for several more hours providing public order patrols until the end of the event. It was only when the large crowds left the racecourse that the crew was stood down and the aircraft returned to its base.

Pilot skills

NPAS pilots work in a high stress, challenging environment where no two days are ever the same and decision making skills are pushed to the limits. The pilots are recruited and employed by NPAS and the service has its own in-house training organisation that can deliver aircraft type rating training.

Finding pilots is a global issue, but that shortage is exacerbated at NPAS where experience has shown that not all pilots are suited to the law enforcement environment. Traditionally, NPAS recruited pilots from the military but that pool has now shrunk; the military working harder to retain pilots and give them longer careers.

The net effect is there is plenty of competition for the type of pilots NPAS needs – Capt Watts said the service is competing with the likes of air ambulance operators for a fairly small pool of experienced pilots. Competition has placed upward pressure on salaries for the type of pilots who fit the profile and can quickly adapt to the unique law enforcement role. He said: "Because we're a single pilot operation we can only recruit experienced pilots as we don't have the ability to bring in a low-hours co-pilot and develop them in-house. We stress it's a highly dynamic, reactive environment and that soon becomes very apparent to them during the training period and when they operate in the police role."

He added that unless they have been in the military or have done some emergency service flying, they are not used to the fact that you could be having a coffee and ten minutes later be airborne and not knowing where you are going or being diverted multiple times en route. The common car chase produces stresses of its own – it can involve trying to get above a fast-moving car: "That car could be moving through multiple airspace or around a busy airport and you've got to negotiate your way through

▼ Seven new H135s have been ordered by the NPAS from Airbus. NPAS

▶ Pilots often operate in heavily populated areas. NPAS

▼ The rotary wing fleet is maintained by Airbus UK. NPAS

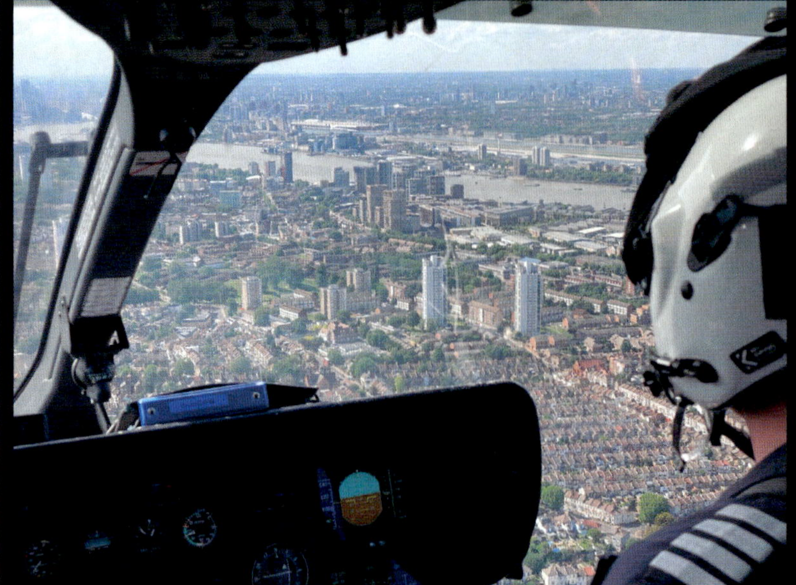

the airspace, through UK weather which often means low-level flying at night. You're operating in an unfamiliar area where you've got to watch your fuel and your diversions and there's just so many things to deal with.

"We have a limited budget and time to train people so we need somebody who's got those core skills; they need to have done something similar before." He said if they haven't had previous experience yet demonstrate a sound set of core skills during selection, "a lot of pilots will not be suited to this type of operation".

The training period for rotary pilots is six to eight weeks and Watts said he makes it clear that even for experienced pilots the learning curve is steep. It is usually

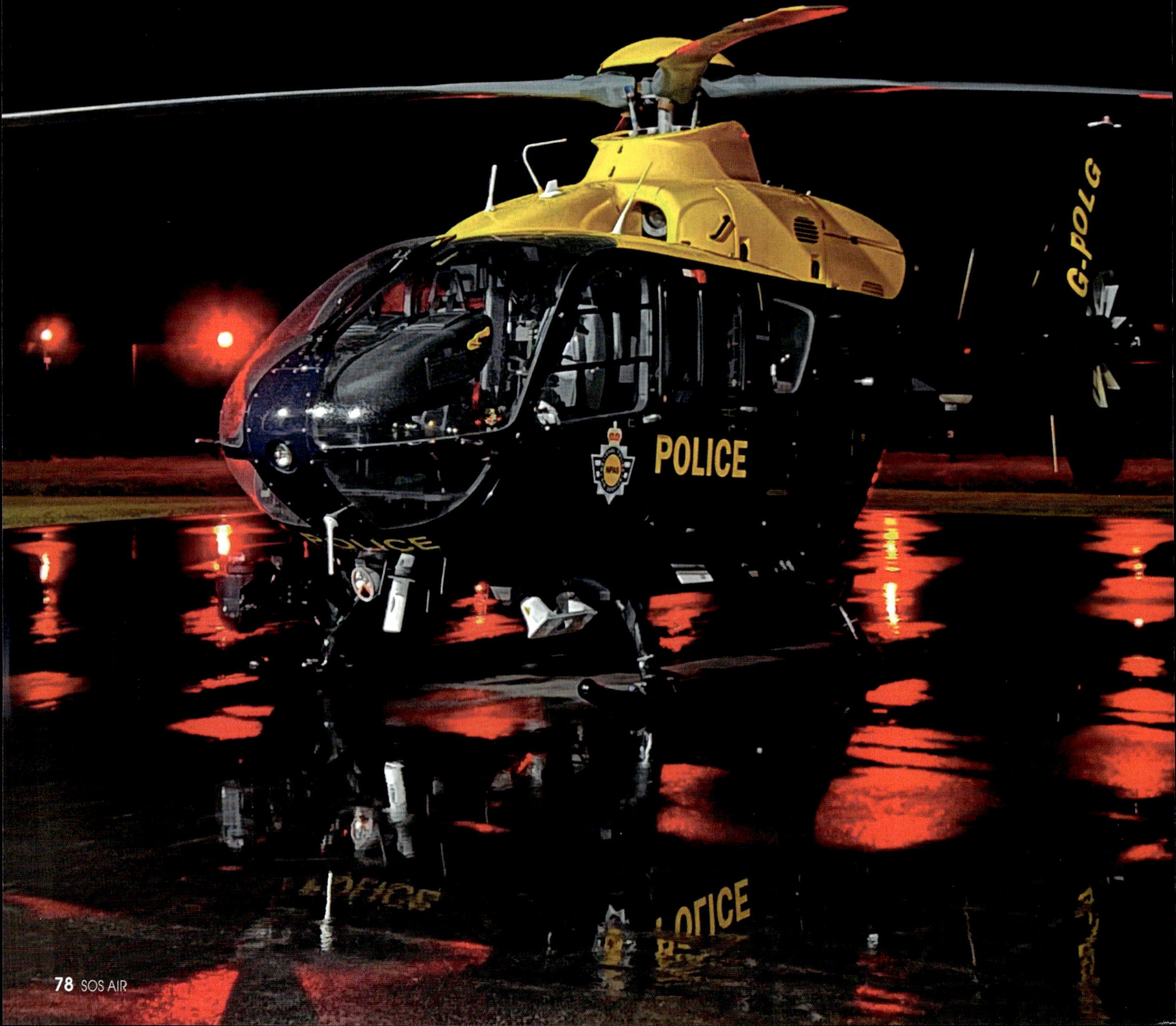

during the night-flying police line training phase that it can become overwhelming for recruits, although he added that with better selection it's now rare for somebody to not get through training: It's also the ability to filter out information when you're listening to three or four police radios as well as air traffic control and it can be quite frantic to tell someone what's going on. You need to sit back from the police operation and be monitoring the aircraft, the systems, the fuel and the weather at the same time you're flying the aircraft and you've got to do that intuitively."

Blending the fleet

In 2024, there were around 32,000 police drone deployments in the UK, so the concept of using drones is not new, although these units were typically very lightweight quadcopter types that can provide a useful search function. Sophisticated uncrewed aerial systems are now available that can carry a camera equivalent to one carried by a crewed aircraft, opening new possibilities that have caught the eye of NPAS.

The service has been appointed to support the development of an application to the UK Civil Aviation Authority for planned flights of beyond visual line of sight uncrewed aircraft. The Schiebel CAMCOPTER S-100 has been selected for the trials with the first test flight scheduled for summer 2025.

Watts described the exercise as a proof of concept trial to determine what are the possible opportunities for drones to move out of the line of sight world into the beyond visual line of sight environment, and operating further, higher and for longer. He added that nobody is doing that yet in the UK and to move into the policing world is a big step: "So we're doing a proof

of concept to really see what is possible with a large drone like the S1 that can carry an MX-10 camera and sensors, radios and ADS-B to see how much of the search function it can do. We're the only operator in the UK that the

CAA has allowed to conduct this type of trial or operation so it's an information gathering exercise for everyone involved."

It has already taken two years to get to this stage and the NPAS team is not expecting to get to

▲ A powerful camera is fitted under the nose of the H135. NPAS

◀ All aircraft must be ready to take off at short notice. NPAS

▼ The four Vulcanair P68Rs operate throughout England and Wales. NPAS

▲ P68Rs are ideal for longer-range patrol missions. NPAS

▶ Searches are involved in the majority of NPAS missions. NPAS

▼ The helicopters carry one pilot and two tactical flight officers. NPAS

the end of the six-month trial and announce it is ready to buy ten drones and introduce them in the next five years. It does expect to have identified the hurdles that need to be overcome to be able to introduce these uncrewed aircraft into service in five to ten years.

Are they safe?

Capt Watts understands the CAA and the public are going to expect the same level of safety from the drones as they do from commercial aircraft; they are not going to accept them crashing into airliners or falling on top of their houses. He said: "These are big 150kg (330lb) aircraft, so the challenge is how do you achieve

that level of safety in the complex and incredibly crowded UK airspace environment, particularly when most of our work goes on in the densely populated areas."

While Watts can see the pitfalls, the long-term aviator is clearly an advocate of drone technology being part of the fleet, safely operating policing missions that suit its capability; he believes there is too much focus on choosing between crewed and uncrewed aircraft as if it's a binary choice: "I see the future will be a blend and it's actually how you co-ordinate and blend the use of crewed and uncrewed aircraft to give the most efficient and effective outcome. It's how you blend the two and use the most effective platform for each task and if you look at it that way it's a slightly different question."

Given that the majority of NPAS missions involve searching for vulnerable or missing people, it's unsurprising that Watts pointed to that activity as one that must transcend any competition or debate about crewed or uncrewed aircraft: "When we're talking about vulnerable missing persons we're talking about people's lives. The amount of risk you're exposing those vulnerable people to is affected by how effective your search platforms are, so you have to leave the `crewed versus uncrewed' politics out of that."

▲ The Vulcanair P68R has a cruise speed of 168kts. NPAS

◄ NPAS is embarking on a fleet renewal programme in 2027. NPAS

▼ NPAS is part of a trial evaluating drone technology. NPAS

Finding the Lost

Seasoned pilots describe search and rescue operations as among their most high-stress missions and there is no doubt that the combination of well-equipped aircraft and trained crews save lives.

Aerial search and rescue is a classic example of using aircraft as force multipliers in emergency situations where eyes in the sky using sophisticated tracking equipment can find people they can't even see. Not only can aircraft detect where lost or injured people are, but specialised crews can be deployed to treat and recover them from locations inaccessible from the ground.

Search and rescue operators use fixed-wing, rotary and uncrewed aircraft that are fitted with an array of mission-specific systems, including night-vison, thermal and video imaging, winches, stretchers and other lifesaving equipment.

They often operate in challenging weather, low visibility or in remote locations day and night, but the combination of aircraft, highly trained pilots and crews and specialised systems are very effective in fulfilling their mission.

Fixed-wing aircraft are commonly used for wide area searches over land or sea where their greater range, extended endurance and sophisticated surveillance equipment allows them to stay on the search longer. A prime example has been the multiple search efforts to locate the Malaysia Airlines 777 airliner that disappeared in 2014 on a flight between Kuala Lumpur and Beijing with the loss of 227 passengers and 12 crew.

A more common incident is searching for yachts in distress or missing on the world's great oceans, where search aircraft will rely on maritime patrol aircraft like the Boeing P-8 Poseidon, Lockheed HC-130 Hercules or similar military aircraft. Finding an upturned yacht with a sailor clinging to a hull in the middle of a raging ocean is a testament to what search and rescue aircraft and their crews can accomplish.

Rotary roles

Helicopters come into their own in environments where agility and the ability to hover or land in confined locations are needed, such as in mountains, forests and inland water sources. Using night-vision systems, thermal imaging and winches, helicopters are the platform from which crews can recover and then treat people while transporting them directly to hospitals.

Unpiloted aerial systems (UAS) or drones are increasingly being used by police and parapublic agencies

▼ **Beechcraft King Airs are used for wide area searches.**
Beechcraft

in search missions, particularly in urban areas where they can be quickly deployed and feed real-time images to ground searchers. Maritime and long-range searches can use larger drones such as the CAMCOPTER S-100, a vertical take-off and land (VTOL) UAS with a range of 125 miles that transmits high-definition images in real time.

A common theme in emergency air services is that the same aircraft types are operating in a range of sectors, but what makes them different is the specialised mission equipment installed on board. Almost any helicopter or aircraft can be used for a simple search with the pilot or observer looking out of the windows, but without the communications and tracking technology it would struggle to fit into the search environment.

The favoured types in search and rescue include Airbus H135, H145 and H175, Bell 412, 429 and 505 and Leonardo AW139 and AW169 aircraft. Fixed-wing aircraft used include the ubiquitous Beechcraft King Air, Pilatus PC-12, Airbus C295 and the Lockheed HC-130.

Firsthand SAR

CHC Helicopters is a global leader in search and rescue (SAR) and operates an extensive and technologically sophisticated network with helicopters, crews and support teams stationed around

▲ Helicopters can deliver help in the most inaccessible areas. Airbus

▼ Leonardo AW139s have the agility and power needed in SAR missions. Leonardo

▲ **Swiss Air-Rescue Riga are specialists in the Swiss Alps.**
Airbus

▼ **New South Wales Police use Bell 412 in SAR and law enforcement roles.**
Bell

the world. It operates SAR bases in Ireland, Norway and Australia and is a significant operator in the offshore energy transportation sector.

One of its contracts in Australia is to provide SAR services to the Royal Australian Air Force (RAAF) at bases that operate fast jets fitted with ejection seats. One of those bases is located 140 miles (222km) from Melbourne at East Sale, the home of RAAF pilot training, using Pilatus PC-21 jets and the RAAF Roulettes aerobatic team.

The high-performance PC-21 is capable of sustained low-level speeds of more than 320kts and can produce fighter-like rates of roll in excess of 200° per second. The RAAF base is located on the coast and to support the operations CHC has one Leonardo AW139 stationed there ready for search and rescue operations whenever the PC-21s are airborne.

The AW139 usually carries a crew of four, two pilots, a hoist operator and a rescue crew member, whose job it is to enter the water or other environments and recover the injured or distressed person. This writer had the rare privilege of joining a training exercise on the CHC AW139 over Victoria's Bass Strait and observed how that happens from the cabin.

A feature of the AW139 is its ability to locate a target, enter the position in the aircraft system and then rely on the automation to make a controlled descent to position it over the target at the right height for recovery to take place.

In the training flight, the pilot picked a spot and a smoke flare was dropped out of the door as a reference point for where the rescue would take place. The pilots engaged the automation and for my benefit took their hands off the controls as the aircraft automatically descended in a loop until arriving directly above the smoke in the hover position.

Wet-stretcher recovery

Ejecting out of a fast-moving jet is not without risk so CHC's recovery procedures are tailored to afford protection for those with spinal injuries, using a process called wet-stretcher winching. This process is used by CHC crews when supporting defence forces and to ensure proficiency it is practised by crews every 90 days.

The rescue crew member deploys from the aircraft with the stretcher, recovers the survivor and places the person on the stretcher in the water; both are then winched back into the aircraft. It is not a simple process, which is why it is a large part of crew training. If sea conditions don't allow the wet-stretcher method then traditional recovery processes are employed.

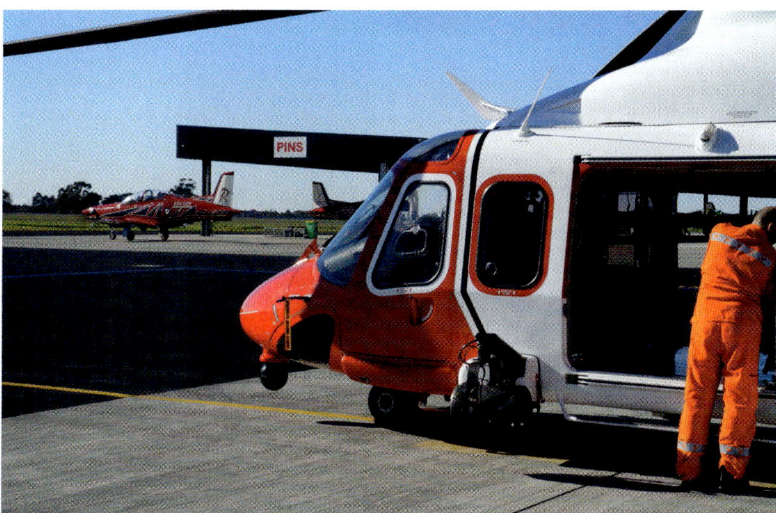

◀ CHC are on call when RAAF Pilatus PC-21s are flying.
Michael Doran

Supporting the RAAF in these situations requires Level 1 SAR support, which means the aircraft and crew are capable of effecting night over-water rescues. This requires an aircraft that has SAR modes enabling it to automatically descend over water at night and recover a person from the water.

In that mode, the crew member can control the aircraft with ten knots authority in all lateral directions as the pilot is effectively hands-off and the tech crew in the back are controlling the aircraft.

New crew enter into a programme to be trained and endorsed to fill both the hoist operator and rescue crew member positions with an initial three-month training period followed at three-monthly and then six-monthly intervals. It generally takes around three years for a crew member to gain the experience and proficiency to move into the hoist operator role.

The crews in CHC's operations in the Irish Sea or northern Norway are subjected to the added danger of freezing cold water immersion, although all crews undertake basic offshore survival training. That involves the fundamentals of helicopter underwater escape training, escaping from low-lit or smoke-filled environments, firefighting and sea survival.

The AW139s carry a range of mission equipment that usually includes a FLIR (forward looking infrared) camera, mission management system and operator console, hoists, searchlights, satellite phone, night-vision imaging system and auxiliary fuel tank.

For air crews there is an array of tools, devices, swimming gear, lights, radio and – most importantly – survival suits. The suit is worn with an inflatable life-vest and features inbuilt gloves, neck-sealing collar, sea-hood, knife pocket and reflective trim and must meet standards adopted by the European Aviation Safety Agency.

Airbus SAR

Airbus Helicopters has a range of aircraft used for SAR missions with many global operators using types including the H135, H145, H175 and H225 Super Puma. While these multi-role aircraft are used on many types of missions, it is in Europe where Airbus has built a strong presence in SAR operations.

In France, the Sécurité Civile civil defence service performs rescue and air medical services with a fleet of four Airbus five-bladed H145s and 33 EC145s. At the end of 2023, the French Armament General Directorate ordered 42 new H145s – 36 destined for the Sécurité Civile and six to be used by the Gendarmerie Nationale, with the latter also holding options for 22 more H145s.

The 36 new-generation H145s will progressively replace the EC145s currently in operation with Sécurité Civile and will be used for rescue and air medical services throughout France. The service operates from 23 bases in France and overseas territories and on average rescues one person every 33 minutes.

▼ CHC operates SAR missions in the far north of Norway
CHC. Helicopters

▲ **CHC AW139 pilots taking a hands-off approach.** Michael Doran

Airbus Helicopters CEO Bruno Even said: "The H145 has already proven its worth with the Sécurité Civile conducting many rescue missions in the difficult mountainous environment of the French Alps."

The five-bladed version of the H145, which was certified by EASA in June 2020, increases the aircraft's useful load by 150kg (330lb) and has a low noise footprint that makes it the quietest helicopter in its class. It has a four-axis autopilot and the Airbus Helionix digital avionics suite, which increase safety and reduce pilot workload.

South Tyrol H135

▼ **SAR crew carry an array of gear and wear sea survival suits.** Michael Doran

Airbus is supporting public safety in Europe's South Tyrol region where its aircraft are being used by mountain rescue teams that operate about 600 missions annually with helicopters. The mountain rescue service is deployed where there are no passable roads in the region. Head of the service, Thomas Hellrigl said: "As well as saving people and animals, we also recover things like drones and paragliders that are trapped in impassable terrain. It's a way to combine our love for the mountains with voluntary work."

Around a third of all rescue missions are carried out by helicopters that provide direct access in places that are difficult or otherwise impossible to access. Airbus H145 and H135 helicopters are used by the service and with the highest peak being 4,000m (13,100ft) high powerful aircraft like these twin-engined Airbus types are needed.

All the aircraft are equipped with a 90m (295ft) cable winch and the mountain services use the H135 to carry out what they call tow searches. These are when a rope is connected to the underside of the helicopter and used to fly rescuers

◀ Leonardo 139s have carved out a strong SAR presence. Avincis

and paramedics to the scene, with rescuers trained in both winch and tow rescue procedures.

There are three heliports in South Tyrol with one of those operated by the Aiut Alpin Dolomites Association, a voluntary association that has been operating in summer and winter since 1985. The helicopter rescue service has been operational from Pontives (Val Gardena) since the summer of 2003 where its headquarters have a night helipad.

In 2015, Aiut Alpin received its current aircraft, a H135 T3, the first of its type delivered by Airbus. The cabin has been fitted out similar to a hospital emergency room by Swiss company Aerolite with equipment including defibrillators, respirator

▼◀ Airbus H225 Super Pumas were early entrants into SAR missions. Airbus

▼ France's Sécurité Civile is adding more Airbus H145s. Airbus

▲ Avincis AW139s are operating SAR missions in Spain. *Avincis*

and ventilator, portable suction units and a medical kit containing equipment for chest drainage, intubation, amputation, reanimation and stabilising the patient.

Spanish SAR

In September 2024, emergency aerial services operator Avincis announced it had been awarded a further five-year contract to provide search and rescue services to Spain's Maritime Safety and Rescue Society (SASEMAR). Avincis has delivered uninterrupted SAR support in the region for the past 30 years and the new €305m (£257m) contract solidifies the company's relationship with the Spanish government agency.

Under the contract, Avincis will continue to carry out search and rescue missions assigned by Salvamento Marítimo from its 11 helicopter bases and along Spain's 4,900m coastline. The service operates 24/7 every day of the year and started in 1993 when the first contract was signed between Avincis and the agency.

By the time the contract was renewed in September 2024, Avincis had flown more than 100,000 hours, completed approximately 16,000 missions and rescued or evacuated more than 8,500 people. John Boag, Group CEO of Avincis said that SASEMAR is one of the company's longest standing and most respected clients and Avincis will continue to be there whenever needed over the next five years.

SASEMAR is tasked with providing public services for the rescue of human life at sea, combatting marine pollution, monitoring and assisting maritime traffic, maritime safety and navigation, tugging and ship assistance as well as other complementary services. Its operational area covers an area of around 580,000m^2 or three times the size of Spain's national territory.

Italian drama

In Italy, Avincis provides helicopter search and rescue, emergency medical, aerial firefighting and different services using unmanned aerial vehicles. It operates from 45 bases around the country and in May 2025 Avincis was called on for a particularly complex rescue operation.

On May 18, 2025, the crew of the Pegaso 2 helicopter, a Leonardo AW139 operated on behalf of the Tuscany region, successfully completed a challenging rescue operation along the rocky coastline of Punta Polveraia on Elba Island.

The challenging terrain was a stretch of cliffs with rock formations directly overlooking the sea, meaning that the pilot of the AW139 had to perform a technical landing directly on the rocks. That allowed the medical personnel to assist a tourist who had suffered a serious medical emergency in a location that was difficult to reach by land.

The technical skill and teamwork of the pilots, hoist operators and qualified medical staff ensured a successful outcome in this high-stakes rescue. Avincis is one of the world's leading critical services operators, saving lives and protecting communities.

▼ Aiut Alpin operates SAR missions with the Airbus EC135. *Airbus*

Its reach extends from headquarters in Lisbon to bases throughout Portugal, Spain, Italy, Norway, Sweden and Finland as well as operations in Chile and Mozambique. It has a fleet of more than 220 rotary and fixed-wing aircraft and a team of some 2,400 highly trained and experienced professionals, including pilots, crews and technicians.

Something different

In February 2025, the US Coast Guard ventured 300 miles off the coast of Hawaii to evacuate a cruise ship passenger who had experienced multiple strokes and needed further medical assessment and care.

The call for help came into the Coast Guard's Joint Rescue Co-ordination Center Honolulu from the *Koningsdam*, a Holland America Line cruise ship. The crew reported that a 72-year-old man experienced multiple stroke episodes offshore of the island of Hawaii.

Coast Guard staff consulted with the duty flight surgeon who recommended a medevac (medical evacuation) within 20 hours and the next morning a HC-130 Hercules airplane crew and an MH-65 Dolphin helicopter crew from Coast Guard Air Station Barbers Point rendezvoused with the *Koningsdam* about 57 miles south of Honolulu.

The helicopter crew safely and successfully hoisted the ailing man from the cruise ship and transported the patient to Queen's Medical Center in Honolulu in a stable condition. Lt Cdr John Stockton, HC-130 Hercules aircraft commander, Air Station Barbers Point, said: "By combining the skills of our crews and the specialised capabilities of our aircraft, we are able to respond to emergencies across the vast Pacific region. Teamwork is critically important for medevacs, which are among the most time-sensitive and high-stakes missions we take on."

The HC-130 Hercules is a versatile and rugged aircraft mainly used by the US Air Force and Coast Guard for search and rescue missions and is derived from the widely used C-130 Hercules. In its military roles its key missions include aerial refuelling of helicopters, combat search and rescue and the recovery of personnel in hostile or remote environments.

The latest Coast Guard version is the HC-130J, which is derived from the Lockheed Martin KC-130J tanker operated by the US Marine Corps and does not have the capability to refuel helicopters in flight. The HC-130Js were heavily modified for the Coast Guard by adding large side windows, sea search radar, a FLIR IR/EO (electro-optical/infrared) sensor and an enhanced communications suite.

The HC-130J also has the Minotaur mission management system and incorporates sensors, radar and command, control and communications, computers, intelligence, surveillance and reconnaissance equipment. That integration allows crews to gather and process information that can be transmitted to other units and platforms during flight.

▲ French Gendarmerie forces are adding new H145s. Airbus

▼ Sikorsky S92s have a place in SAR operations. Sikorsky

Border
Watchdogs

More than 200 fixed wing, rotary and unmanned aircraft operated by US Customs and Border Protection and its Air and Marine Operations unit are monitoring America's frontier.

▲ **US CBP protects the nation's borders from illegal entry.** US CBP

In most countries protecting citizens and securing borders are one of the highest priorities of government, with geopolitical changes in recent years sharpening the focus on how this is being achieved. Protecting borders was once centred on travellers at airports and sea ports, but the undocumented and illegal mass movement of people has radically changed that.

Those tasked with keeping borders secure have to stringently protect thousands of miles of land and sea borders with far more attention than was previously necessary. That responsibility has not changed, but the pressure to perform has, with politicians, the media and the

▶ **Sikorsky Black Hawks operate multiple AMO mission types.** US CBP

public expecting frontline operatives to stem the tide of people and illicit goods crossing the border.

While there is a lot of focus on the border between the United States and Mexico and Canada, border protection agencies are struggling to keep up in the Mediterranean, Asia-Pacific, North Africa, the English Channel and throughout South America and the Caribbean. Border protection agencies are employing state of the art technologies on the ground and in the air, with rotary, fixed wing and unmanned aircraft at the forefront. The variety of aircraft and the sophistication of operations are constantly evolving as agencies use these assets to stay one step ahead of narcotics and human traffickers, illegal migrants and suspect sea, land and air incursions.

In many countries these missions are undertaken by military forces, while others rely on government authorities or parapublic operators, such as US Customs and Border Protection, Australia's Border Force, Canada's Border Services Agency and the Royal Canadian Mounted Police.

Securing the US

US Customs and Border Protection (CBP) is the largest federal law enforcement agency of the Department of Homeland Security. As the country's primary border control agency, it is charged with keeping terrorists and their weapons out of the US while facilitating lawful international travel and trade.

In 2024, CBP had more than 60,000 employees performing roles in customs, immigration, border security and agricultural protection. They are tasked with protecting the US through land and air environments against illegal entry, illicit activity or other threats to uphold national sovereignty and promote national and economic security. At more than 300 ports of entry, CBP officers have a complex mission that includes inspecting all foreign visitors, returning US citizens and imported cargo that crosses the border. The United States Border Patrol (USBP) and Air and Marine Operations (AMO) are the uniformed law enforcement components of CBP, responsible for securing US borders between ports of entry.

AMO comprises more than 1,800 federal agents and mission support personnel operating throughout the US, Puerto Rico and US Virgin Islands. It interdicts unlawful people and cargo approaching US borders, investigates criminal networks, provides certain domain awareness in the air and maritime environments and responds to contingencies and national taskings. A spokesperson said that, in 2024, AMO enforcement actions resulted in 1,009 arrests and the apprehension of 48,609 illegal aliens, as well as the seizure or disruption of 244,781lb of cocaine, 2,235lb of fentanyl, 3,061lb of

▲ Black Hawks regularly protect US cities and venues. US CBP

▼ Major sports events are held under the watchful eye of CBP. US CBP

▲ AMO has a fleet of 77 fixed-wing aircraft. US CBP

methamphetamine, 1,499 weapons and $12.5m in cash.

AMO is the world's largest civilian aviation and maritime law enforcement agency and its fleet is often said to be bigger than many of the world's air forces. In April 2025 it was operating a fleet of 216 aircraft, including 77 fixed wing, 131 rotary wing and eight unmanned aircraft. To put that in perspective, the AMO fleet is around the same size as AirAsia (225 aircraft), Qatar Airways (256) and Emirates (269), but not as large as British Airways (301), Alaska Airlines (326), easyJet (358), Southwest Airlines (814), United Airlines (1,483) and American Airlines (1,592). AMO has 107 aircraft in the southwest region, 37 in the southeast, 35 in the northern region and 37 with National Security Operations, including the eight unmanned aircraft. The fleet includes seven fixed wing aircraft types, two helicopter models and the MQ-9 Unmanned Aircraft System, although the agency does not disclose how many of each type are deployed.

Fixed-wing fleet

The seven fixed-wing AMO aircraft range in size from a Cessna C206H single engine light aircraft to a four engine Lockheed Martin P-3 Airborne Early Warning (AEW) and the Lockheed Martin P-3 Long Range Tracker.

AMO operates Cessna C206Hs and T206H Stationairs on surveillance, tracking and reconnaissance missions in support of investigative and enforcement efforts. The aircraft are also used to transport personnel, equipment and evidence and have proven their value in both urban and remote rural areas.

Cessnas are crewed by a pilot and a tactical flight officer to manage and analyse data coming from an electro-optical camera, mapping system and video recording and downlink equipment. These roles and equipment are typical of many aerial law enforcements operations globally, where the tracking technology efficiently and quickly locates and follows targets while relaying intelligence to ground based teams, as well as collecting vital hard evidence to be used in subsequent prosecutions.

AMO's Cessna C206s have a maximum speed of 151kt, a range of 730nm and a service ceiling of 15,700ft, which makes them effective for covert surveillance and reconnaissance. With a maximum speed of 162kt, a range of 1,000nm and ceiling of 27,000ft, the added performance of the T206 Turbo Stationairs is available when AMO is looking for something more than a 206H can provide.

▼ The Black Hawk's large cabin is ideal for medevac services. US CBP

▲ An AMO Black Hawk patrolling the US-Canada border.
US CBP

◄ Air and Marine Operations has more than 200 aircraft.
US CBP

▲ The Black Hawk's size helps with natural disaster missions. US CBP

▼ AMO's Pilatus PC-12 operates covert surveillance and tracking. US CBP

When performing similar missions, AMO can also call on the Pilatus PC-12 single engine turboprop, which can fly for four hours at up to 30,000ft and cover 1,040nm at a maximum speed of 236kt. These are primarily used for surveillance over land or the relocation of personnel and equipment. What sets the PC-12 apart is its combination of the slow speed capability of a Cessna 210 with the high speed and payload of a Beechcraft King Air. This is especially useful when conducting covert tracking and surveillance missions that require stand-off range from the target to avoid counter detection. It is fitted with a forward-looking detection system that senses infrared radiation created by objects warmer or colder than the surrounding ambient temperature.

The Beechcraft Super King 350ER is a twin engine medium range multi-role enforcement aircraft that conducts aerial patrols and surveillance over land and water. It has a crew of two pilots and two sensor operators who manage the state-of-the-art sensors and video recorders that document suspect activities for evidentiary use. The Super King is an optimal platform for enhanced law enforcement missions and can be rapidly reconfigured to carry personnel and cargo ifn required. It has maximum speed of 220kt, a range of 1,200nm and a service ceiling altitude of 35,000ft, the highest of any aircraft in the AMO fleet.

Keeping costs down

Bombardier Dash 8 turboprops are a regular sight at regional airports worldwide and the smaller variants, such as the Q200 and Q300, are finding new lives in a variety of sectors, including as firefighting tankers and as patrol aircraft with AMO. In airline settings the Q200 was typically configured to carry up to 39 passengers and the Q300 up to 56 passengers.

The AMO Dash 8s have a maximum speed of 242kt, a range of 1,600nm and fly up to a ceiling of 25,000ft. The twin turboprops can operate for up to six to seven hours and are equipped with multimode radar and EO/IR sensors that can detect and track maritime and surface targets. They are also fitted with SeaVue marine search radar that can detect small targets from operational altitudes to increase surveillance coverage and accuracy from fixed-wing, rotary and uncrewed aircraft. The Dash 8 has the lowest per hour cost of any AMO aircraft and is ideal for responding to natural disasters or other emergencies.

The agency operates two variants of the Lockheed Martin P-3 platform: the P-3 Airborne Early Warning (AEW) aircraft and the P-3 Long Range Tracker (LRT). Both have a range of 4,000nm, 12 hours endurance and a service ceiling of 28,000ft, while the AEW has a maximum speed of 330kt and the LRT is significantly faster at 404kt.

The AEW performs a wide variety of missions and is the first choice for operations that require long station time overhead, hemispheric range and flights in inclement weather and environmental conditions. It is often useds in tandem with the P-3 LRT, where its strengths lie in detecting and tracking multiple targets using AN/APS-145 radar and EO/IO sensors. When paired, the P-3 AEW detects and tracks multiple targets and the accompanying LRT intercepts, identifies and tracks them.

The P-3 is the only dedicated law enforcement AEW aircraft in the world and was developed as a force multiplier in joint operations with federal, state and local partners for national security events. It carries a crew of two pilots, a flight engineer and five radar/sensor operators and can operate from 8,000ft runways. It is routinely sent on temporary duty to support the US government and allied initiatives to stem smuggling into the United States.

The P-3 LRT is primarily used for high-endurance, all-weather

tactical missions including long range patrols and surveillance along US borders and in drug transit zones in Central and South America. It is fitted with EO/IR sensors that allow crews to maintain awareness of targets, APG-66 radar for detection and SeaVue marine search radar.

Black Hawks fit best

For the US Customs and Border protection agency there can be no higher profile mission than securing the southern border with Mexico, where it joins with other security agencies to stem the flow of migrants trying to enter the country illegally. In those hot, dusty and harsh environments, the arrival of AMO agents is often signalled by the unmistakable sound of Sikorsky UH-60 Black Hawk helicopters.

AMO operates Black Hawks with a maximum cruise speed of 150kts, a range of 600nm, four hours endurance and a flight ceiling of 20,000ft. The aircraft are fitted with auxiliary fuel tanks, EO/IR sensors, a night sun spotlight and are fully compatible with night-vision goggle operations.

The Black Hawks are the frontline of the AMO's mission to protect the US public from threats of terrorism and drug smuggling, as well as providing aerial security and an ominous presence over critical venues and major urban events, such as the NFL Super Bowl. The spacious cabin and onboard equipment mean they are well suited for search and rescue missions over land and sea, emergency evacuations, disaster support and medevac services.

The UH-60 is a large, powerful aircraft that has a maximum take-off weight of 22,000lb and an empty weight of 12,500lb. It is crewed by two pilots and one or more crew members and can carry 11 seated passengers,

▲ The CBP aircraft are deployed on humanitarian operations. US CBP

▼ AMO fields the P-3 Early Warning Aircraft. US CBP

▲ **An AMO ground team air co-ordinator (GTAC).** US CBP

six stretchers or 9,000lb of external cargo. The power of the Black Hawk means it does not sacrifice speed and range to perform missions such as maritime, aviation and land interdiction, insertion of agents into remote areas and joint operations during contingency operations and national taskings.

The UH-60 also has excellent capability to conduct search and rescue operations because of its hoist and large cabin, which allows crew to recover, assess and stabilise injured people. They are also workhorses with the strength to carry heavy external loads to move equipment and personnel to remote locations and deplane agents with fast-rope operations.

Effective alternatives

Not every AMO mission requires the size and capabilities of a Black Hawk. Sometimes a smaller, lighter helicopter can be a better fit for law enforcement and surveillance operations. It deploys the Airbus H125 Light Enforcement Helicopter (LEH) for aerial patrols and surveillance of stationery or moving targets.

The H125 is a member of Airbus' rugged and proven Ecureuil family, which includes the AS350, AS355, AS550, AS555, H125, H125M, EC130 and H130. More than 7,200 have been delivered to more than 2,600 operators in 137 countries. In North America, the H125 was formerly known as the AStar AS350.

AMO operates the type with a two-person crew that consists of a pilot and sensor operator to provide an aerial surveillance platform in metropolitan areas. Similar to civilian law enforcement agencies, the AMO H125 is fitted with an infrared detection system, digital moving map, tactical searchlight, EO/IR infrared camera and is compatible with night-vision goggle operations.

The aircraft also has video downlink capabilities to provide intelligence and communications support that enhances officer safety during high risk operations and increase stealth during surveillance operations. The onboard video recorders document suspect activities, such as subjects fleeing or disposing of evidence, which

▼ **The AMO Airbus AS350s help protect US borders.** US CBP

are invaluable in subsequent investigations and court cases.

A bold future

Unmanned aircraft systems (UAS) are tailor-made for border patrols and surveillance tasks, so its unsurprising that AMO has been using them for some time. A spokesperson said there are eight systems deployed on national security operations with the agency, operating the MQ-9 Predator B UAS manufactured by US company General Atomics.

The MQ-9 is used to increase domain awareness to detect, classify, monitor and respond to threats at the nation's borders and approaches to the US. The UAS has a maximum speed of 240kt and can fly at altitudes up to 50,000ft, with up to 20 hours endurance.

AMO deploys the multi-purpose aircraft to aid in disaster relief and emergency response efforts co-ordinated with Department of Homeland Security partners, including the Federal Emergency Management Agency and the US Coast Guard. The drone is equipped with electro-optical and infrared sensors, as well as a Vehicle and Dismount Exploitation Radar (VADER) sensor, ground moving target indicator and SeaVue marine search radar.

VADER is a strategic and tactical operations sensor that provides comprehensive situational awareness for an expanded area. Incorporating it in a UAS helps operators to detect moving targets and perform coherent change detection.

The large payload of the Predator B allows for more sensors to be installed and was part of the decision-making process when CBP selected the system. It was first used along the southern border with Mexico and was later deployed along the northern border with Canada and beyond.

The Predator B has a wingspan of 66ft and is 36ft long with a gross maximum take-off weight of 10,500lb. It has an internal payload of 850lb and an external payload of 3,000lb and is powered by a Honeywell TPE331-10 powerplant. It can be remotely piloted or operate fully autonomously and is fitted with a Ku-Band beyond-line-of-sight SATCOM dat link control.

▲ AMO has 131 helicopters in its 2025 fleet. US CBP

▼ AMO operates smaller fast aircraft on tracking and reconnaissance missions. US CBP

The Uncrewed Future

Emergency services worldwide are being pushed to do more with less and in almost every field, uncrewed aerial systems are either already in use or are being trialled.

▶ Sikorsky first demonstrated its pilotless UH Black Hawk helicopter in 2022; it was controlled from 300 miles away. Sikorsky

▼ In 2025, Sikorsky teamed with US technology company Rain to demonstrate the pilotless Black Hawk. Sikorsky

By their very nature, emergency missions can be both challenging and dangerous and cannot always operate at night or in severe flying environments. They are also very expensive to operate so for all those reasons it is not surprising that unmanned systems are finding their way into emergency aviation.

As the following story shows, uncrewed aerial systems (UAS) are adding new equipment into the toolbox of public safety agencies, just as helicopters did decades ago, in firefighting, law enforcement, border protection, search and rescue and emergency medical missions.

UAS manufacturers are developing aircraft and systems that are designed to support the traditional methods, rather than suggesting that everything can be operated by remote control. In fighting wildfires, drones can be invaluable as first responders to spot fires and relay pictures and data in real time to controllers, allowing them to marshal appropriate resources to prevent small fires turning into catastrophic events.

In an alpine area where changing weather conditions can ground aircraft, the uncrewed system can still fly and use its thermal imaging camera to find people, ferry vital medicines or supplies and safely guide rescuers to the right location.

Police and other law enforcement agencies can quickly deploy a drone fitted with an array of cameras to a reported crime scene to gain intelligence and situational awareness. That allows officers heading to the incident to see what is unfolding in real time and plan their mission in a safer and more effective way.

So whether it is a Black Hawk helicopter without a pilot, a small drone operated in the field or a sophisticated uncrewed eVTOL (electric vertical take-off and landing) aircraft, all of them will be making a vital difference to emergency missions and saving lives now and in the future.

Pilotless Black Hawk

The Black Hawk helicopter is one of the most rugged and recognisable aircraft in the world so why it is appearing in this section on unmanned aircraft? The fact is that the Black Hawk is undergoing extensive trials by

both military and civilian operators for pilotless aviation, including emergency missions.

Sikorsky, the manufacturer of Black Hawks, started demonstrating unmanned flights to the US Army in 2022 by proving that the aircraft could safely and reliably perform internal and external cargo resupply missions without humans on board.

The Black Hawk is fitted with the Sikorsky Innovations MATRIX flight autonomy system that allows for assisted flight handling for two pilot operations, virtual co-pilot for a single pilot or fully autonomous flight with no pilots. In 2024, Sikorsky demonstrated how the aircraft could be operated by one person using a tablet computer 300 miles away to take off, hover, fly a circuit and land the helicopter.

Autonomous detection and firefighting

Taking things to the next level, Sikorsky, a Lockheed Martin company, has teamed up with US technology business Rain, which is a leader in autonomous aerial wildfire containment technology. Rain's technology is helping fire agencies more quickly suppress wildfires during the earliest stages of ignition.

In November 2024, the two successfully demonstrated how an autonomous Black Hawk can be commanded to take off, identify the location and size of a small fire and then accurately drop water from an external bucket slung 60ft below the aircraft to suppress the flames.

To demonstrate the precision and accuracy of the autonomous system, the Black Hawk made three successive water drops that extinguished a 12in diameter propane-fuelled fire ring emitting a six-inch tall flame. The system also rapidly adjusted the flight path to account for an eight to 10kts crosswind during each drop.

Rain CEO Maxwell Brodie said government agencies, aerial firefighting operators and investors are coming together to learn how both flight and mission autonomy can help prevent high-intensity, million-acre wildfires. He said: "Wildfires cost the US over $390bn (£294bn) annually and multiple risk factors are set to grow up to

▲ Draganfly drones can be used in conditions unsafe for aircraft. Draganfly

▲ Drones are a quick way to deliver essential supplies in an emergency. Draganfly

▲▶ Camcopter S-100 UAS are used for maritime surveillance in Europe. Schiebel

▼ The autonomous Black Hawk successfully detected and extinguished a simulated fire. Sikorsky

30% by 2030. We look forward to demonstrating to lawmakers how autonomous aircraft can stop wildfires from breaking out or continue the fight into the night and in turbulent and smoky conditions, where crewed aircraft wouldn't venture."

The demonstration was witnessed by representatives from the National Aeronautics and Space Administration, the US Federal Emergency Management Agency, Los Angeles County Fire Department, Orange County Fire Authority and investors. It was held as part of a two-day wildlands firefighting meeting to discuss autonomy.

The 30-minute flight was commanded by guests using a handheld tablet and although there were Sikorsky safety pilots in the Black Hawk monitoring the controls, they remained hands-off until the aircraft landed.

After the demonstration, Igor Cherepinsky, director of Sikorsky Innovations, said: "With Rain's software loaded onto the aircraft and a tablet, wildland firefighters in the field could deploy autonomous Black Hawk or Firehawk helicopters to search and attack wildfires before they spread out of control. Our two companies are ready to demonstrate the joint capability in more dynamic conditions chosen by firefighters."

Draganfly drone difference

For more than two decades, Canada's Draganfly has created high-quality, cutting-edge drone solutions, software and AI systems that have revolutionised how organisations operate and serve their stakeholders. It provides drone solutions that define industry standards in markets as diverse as public safety, security, agriculture, mapping, surveying and industrial inspection.

In the public safety sector, Draganfly's industry-leading products are used across the full spectrum of emergency services, including firefighting, search and rescue, border patrol, law

enforcement, medical, disaster response and emergency delivery missions.

While the extensive range of drones produced by Draganfly are impressive in their own right, it is the way they are used and integrated into emergency situations as first responders, intelligence gatherers and support aircraft that best demonstrate what drones can bring to these missions.

On that point, Draganfly chief operating officer Paul Mullen said that while manned aircraft are incredibly safe they still carry some level of risk, especially in difficult environments like wildfires, search and rescue and law enforcement.

That's when the Draganfly drone can act as a force multiplier to take people out of the loop and free up aircraft to focus on other critical areas. He said: "Certainly, a drone as a first responder is an area where we see significant growth, typically in urban policing scenarios and search and rescue by groups that need to make the most out of their dollars, as drones are not as expensive as traditional manned aircraft.

"The other growth area is the prevention side. If you think about the phases of these events you have opportunities for prevention, you have requirements for intervention and then subsequently you have recovery efforts."

In early 2025, Canada endured massive flooding and wildfires in British Columbia, which Mullen uses as an example of the role drones can play in those three phases. They can be used to map floodplains using LIDAR or other sensors and inspect power line infrastructure for vegetation ingress to be able to proactively mitigate fire risk.

If an emergency situation arises, the drone can detect hot spots, deliver fire retardants or materials to those impacted and provide real-time intelligence to controllers on the ground or in the air. Gathering accurate information is the first step towards post-event recovery and

▲ Camcopter S-100 aircraft are ideal for long-range reconnaissance.
Schiebel

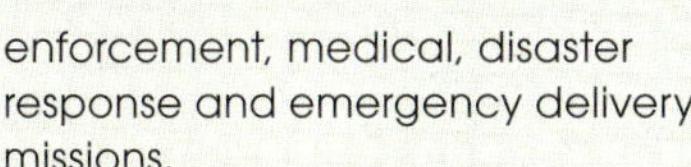

▼ Draganfly drones safely provide valuable intelligence to firefighters.
Draganfly

▶ **Firefighters are using drones to see where assets need to be deployed.** Draganfly

again a drone can do that quickly and efficiently, as Mullen described: "A big part of recovery after a flood, fire or an earthquake will be inspecting infrastructure to ensure it's safe and we see a really big role the drone can play there. You have both an asset that can complement existing efforts as well as taking a very holistic approach to mitigating or resolving risk during and after an incident."

Helicopters play a significant role in urban law enforcement and using them to covertly monitor situations or follow fleeing vehicles and offenders is often a feature seen on the evening news. Drones equipped with high-quality cameras are an effective tool when deployed to a scene before first responders arrive, providing situational awareness so officers can safely prepare for whatever awaits them at the scene.

"Currently, it's still new and we've really seen that market mature over the last three to five years and they are becoming more and more common," said Mullen. "The drone has proven to be a real tool to increase situational awareness and add a different mechanism for intervention to help responders protect the public in a safer fashion."

Similar to other emergency agencies, the medical field has supplemented traditional road vehicles with helicopter and fixed-wing aircraft and is now exploring what drones can offer. Those use cases have included drones delivering a defibrillator to an urban emergency, sending medicines in a temperature-controlled container to a remote area in Canada or collecting medical tests in the middle of the Australian outback.

During Canada's 2023 wildfire season, the Draganfly Service Team deployed its technology to detect hot spots across six locations in British Columbia. The aim was to use drones to provide early detection capabilities to combat fires before they became catastrophic.

The Draganfly team used UAVs fitted with thermal cameras to conduct aerial reconnaissance missions and provide the precise temperature measurements crucial for identifying hotspots. The drone also carried zoom and RGB cameras for context and navigation while a laser range finder assisted in distance measurement, which is critical for assessing fire proximity.

The drones surveyed the landscape for signs of heat anomalies and when a hot spot was detected the team immediately relayed that to firefighting units, allowing crews to contain the fires before they spread further. Using the Draganfly UAVs, more than 1,000 hot spots were identified and addressed, saving an estimated CAN$2m (£1.1m) in firefighting resources.

▼ **Schiebel is a world leader in unmanned aerial systems.** Schiebel

CAMCOPTER works 24/7

Founded in Austria in 1951, the Schiebel Group has built an international reputation for producing high-tech military, commercial and humanitarian products, including the revolutionary CAMCOPTER S-100 unmanned air system (UAS).

The CAMCOPTER is a VTOL unit that can take off and land virtually anywhere without the need for any supporting equipment and operate day or night in adverse weather conditions. It has a beyond line of sight capability of 124 miles over land and sea up to a service ceiling of 18,000ft in a typical configuration.

Significantly, it can operate in environments where GPS is not available with missions planned and controlled via a simple point-and-click graphical user interface. The S-100 can carry a 75lb payload up to ten hours and is powered with Avgas or JP-5 heavy fuel.

The CAMCOPTER's versatility is finding a home in emergency aviation in a variety of missions, including aerial law enforcement, search and rescue, maritime surveillance and emission monitoring. The S-100's ability to fly slowly and hover makes it ideally suited to law enforcement and maritime operations.

The CAMCOPTER S-100 is being operated by more than 40 customers worldwide, including the Royal Navy, and in 2025 Schiebel had its multi-year contract with the European Maritime Safety Agency (EMSA) extended for the third time. The contract is for service provision with remotely piloted aircraft systems (RPAS) for supporting EU member states in maritime surveillance and emission monitoring missions.

The contract began in 2018 and since then the S-100 has conducted more than 1,780 deployment days for EMSA across Europe, including in Croatia, France, Finland, Denmark, Spain, Estonia, Romania, Lithuania, Iceland, Germany and Belgium.

The CAMCOPTER is stationed either on land or ships at sea conducting general night and day maritime surveillance, search and rescue operations, and oil spill detection, as well as monitoring the sulphur content of ship's emissions to ensure compliance with the limits set by the International Maritime Organisation.

In the UK, the National Police Air Service (NPAS) provides 24/7 borderless air support to police forces across England and Wales from a national network of operational bases. In 2025. NPAS selected Schiebel to support its most ambitious trial of beyond visual line of sight (BVLOS) uncrewed aircraft operations.

The trial is studying the feasibility of using uncrewed aerial

▼ Sikorsky is developing a new unmanned system that is both helicopter and airplane. Sikorsky

▲ Sikorsky's 'rotor blown wing' transitions between vertical and horizontal flight.
Sikorsky

▼▶ The EH-216F uses cannisters to penetrate windows, delivering dry powder and extinguishing a fire.
EHang

▼▶▶ The EHang 216F is powered by 16 electric motors driving 16 propellers with a top speed of 80mph. EHang

▼ EHang has extensively trialled the firefighting EH216F, which can reach altitudes up to 1,968ft. EHang

innovative new uncrewed aerial system aircraft that operates in both helicopter and airplane modes.

In March 2025, Sikorsky Innovations successfully validated the advanced control laws to fly a 'rotor blown wing' (RBW) UAS, a flying-wing aircraft that takes off and lands vertically in a tail-sitter configuration. The 115lb twin prop-rotor prototype is powered by batteries and has the potential to be scaled to larger sizes requiring hybrid-electric propulsion.

In little more than a year, Sikorsky Innovations has progressed through preliminary design, simulation,

systems to operate alongside crewed police helicopters and aeroplanes in support of police operations. Schiebel will be flying the S-100 in a selected and controlled environment to assess UAS capabilities as part of a concept for a future blended fleet operated by NPAS.

The aim of the trial is to understand if advancements in aviation technology can bring benefits to policing and be safely introduced into UK airspace. NPAS head of futures and innovations David Walters said the organisation is evaluating how it might integrate uncrewed aircraft into its existing CAA (Civil Aviation Authority) approved operating model. He said: "We cannot predict the outcome of the trial, but it is imperative we deliver the same, or improved, capability that we have today with our crewed aircraft. The desired outcome is to be able to offer police forces in England and

Wales a way of supporting their operations in an even more flexible way, with a continued emphasis on public safety."

The trial will run in the South West of England, away from built-up environments, from summer 2025. NPAS has spent two years building a robust safety case to ensure the trial can operate safely and with minimum disruption to the public and other airspace users.

If successful, the CAMCOPTER will potentially be used on a variety of missions ranging from high-risk missing people and vehicle pursuits to firearms containments, public order and crowd control, intelligence gathering, counter-terrorism, major incidents and aerial searches.

Sikorsky's helicopter airplane

While Sikorsky is pioneering unmanned flight in its Black Hawk helicopter, it is also developing an

tethered and untethered flight to gather aerodynamic and flight control data. Sikorsky Innovations director Igor Cherepinsky said new control laws were required for the transition manoeuvre to work seamlessly and efficiently: "Our rotor blown wing has demonstrated the control power and unique qualities necessary to transition repeatedly and predictably from a hover to high-speed wing-borne cruise flight and back again. The data indicates we can operate from pitching ships' decks and unprepared ground when scaled to much larger sizes."

Sikorsky sees applications for the RBW in areas such as search and rescue, firefighting monitoring, humanitarian response and pipeline surveillance, while larger variants will enable long-range reconnaissance and piloted drone teaming (crewed/uncrewed) missions.

The company is also developing a 1.2mW hybrid-electric demonstrator (HEX) configured with a tilt wing and a fuselage to carry passengers and cargo on long-distance flights. It expects to have a HEX power system test bed ready to demonstrate hover capability in 2027.

In January 2025, the 10.3ft composite wingspan aircraft completed more than 40 take-offs and landings and performed 30 transitions between helicopter and airplane modes, which are the most complex manoeuvre demanded of the UAS, and reached a top cruise speed of 86kts.

EHang leading the way

China is trailblazing urban air mobility and in March 2025 its aviation regulator, the Civil Aviation Administration of China (CAAC,) granted the world's first air operator

▼ EHang's autonomous EH-216F is a firefighting eVTOL that can quickly respond to high-rise fires. EHang

▲ The autonomous EH-216 can be used on a range of emergency missions in all environments.
EHang

certificates (AOCs) for civil human-carrying pilotless aerial vehicles. Granting the AOCs was the final link in a three-part process that has opened the way for commercialising low-altitude human-carrying flight services in China.

The certificates were granted to Guangdong EHang General Aviation (EHang) and its joint venture company Hefei HeYi Aviation. The AOCs clear the way for customers to buy flight tickets for low-altitude tourism, urban sightseeing and other diverse human-carrying flight services at sites in the Chinese cities of Guangzhou and Hefei.

Obtaining an air operator certificate is no mean feat and is

the culmination of a process that has seen EHang granted the world's first type certificate (TC), standard airworthiness certificate (AC) and production certificate (PC) for its EH216-S pilotless human-carrying eVTOL aircraft.

EHang is positioning the EH216 series to meet the needs of various markets, including passenger transportation, logistics, aerial media and Smart City management. The EH216S eVTOL is now ready to operate commercial air taxi routes and aerial sightseeing while EHang is also offering alternate versions of the autonomous aircraft for emergency rescue and logistics operations.

High-rise firefighter

In 2021, EHang operated the pilotless EH216 and EH216F firefighting eVTOL in a high-rise building firefighting and emergency rescue exercise in China. The dispatched aircraft successfully completed tasks including fire detection, aerial broadcasting, breaking windows and extinguishing fires, rescuing trapped people and airdropping essential supplies.

The EH216F can reach altitudes of up to 600m (1,968ft) with a payload of 100 litres (26.4 gallons) of firefighting material and is fitted with six fire projectiles filled with ABC superfine dry extinguishing powder that can penetrate a window to

▼ EHang envisions using the EH216 for delivering medical and health supplies.
EHang

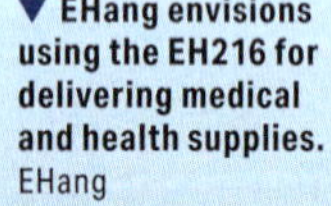

deposit the powder directly on the fire and smother it.

The aircraft is fitted with a zoom camera that enables firefighters to quickly identify the location of the fire and has a high pressure nozzle that can be pointed directly at the fire to shoot firefighting foam or water-based liquid. The EH216F also has a laser-aiming device for accurate dispersion and can operate in smoky conditions, high temperatures, wind and rain.

The operational plan is to have EH216-Fs deployed in multiple fire stations in cities to react to all high-rise building fires with a radius of three kilometres (1.86 miles) around each station. When the alarm is raised the eVTOL takes off directly from the fire station to quickly fly to any point within its range to begin firefighting or other tasks as necessary.

The unit has a visible light 10x zoom camera that enables firefighters to quickly identify the location and extent of the fire within the high-rise building remotely and respond accordingly. It is envisaged that each location would have an eVTOL fleet ready to quickly attack fires and the EH216F has been approved by the China National Firefighting Equipment Quality Supervision Testing Center.

The aircraft is powered by 16 electric motors driving 16 propellers that generate a maximum speed of 80mph and a flying time of 21 minutes with a maximum payload of 220kg (495lb). The EH216F is 7.33m (24.5ft) long, 5.61m (18.75ft) wide and has a height of 2.2m (7.7ft); it can be fully charged in under two hours.

In December 2024, EHang announced plans to open a national headquarters for its low-altitude emergency rescue equipment in Beijing that will

position the area as a hub for the emergency rescue industry and a pilot demonstration zone for related new technologies.

The Beijing Low-Altitude Safety Emergency Industrial Park is being established in partnership with the local district government and they will also establish a comprehensive Emergency Firefighting Industrial Park in the district. That will serve as a site for research and development, testing, manufacturing, sales, maintenance and training for the EH216F.

The two parties will collaborate to develop a range of low-altitude emergency mission scenarios in the Beijing Fangshan District, including urban firefighting, forest fire extinguishing, industrial emergency rescue, inspection and disaster relief. They have also agreed to explore and develop applications including logistics transportation, cultural tourism sightseeing and passenger transportation.

Spanish connection

EHang is keen to see its eVTOLs operating internationally and, while there are regulatory processes to navigate, it is planning to certify and operate the E216 in countries including Thailand, Indonesia, Brazil, Japan and the United Arab Emirates.

The company has already forged strong links with Spain dating back to 2021 when it announced a collaboration with the Spanish National Police and the Polytechnic University of Valencia to explore emergency and security missions using autonomous aerial vehicles (AAVs).

In 2022, the EH216 completed its maiden flight by the Spanish National Police (SNP) at the National Academy of Police in Ávila, Spain. The SNP was the first security institution in the European Union to operate an AAV and said unmanned aircraft systems constitute an alternative technological asset for multiple purposes.

The SNP plans to use the aircraft for missions including accessing contaminated areas with nuclear, radiological, bacteriological or chemical risks, landing in confined

▲ EHang is partnering with Spain's National Police to operate the EH-216 in security missions. EHang

▼ China's EHang has been granted the world's first AOC for an autonomous people-carrying UAS. EHang

areas, aerial logistics and other police services.

In Spain, EHang has forged strategic alliances with the national air navigation service provider ENAIRE, the world's leading airport operator AENA, Aeroports de Catalunya, the SNP and other technology leaders. It is also an active participant in the European Commission's Single European Sky initiative (SESAR).

EHang has established a European Urban Air Mobility (UAM) Centre in Spain – the first of its kind in Europe – and extends the company's reach into Europe, Latin America and Africa. This is part of a strategy to build a global presence and make autonomous, eco-friendly urban air mobility accessible worldwide.

UAS firefighter with 13 propellers

A second Chinese manufacturer is making a move into aerial firefighting using eVTOL aircraft. With dual headquarters in China and Germany, AutoFlight is a technology-driven start-up dedicated to advancing electric aerial vehicles for logistics and urban air mobility solutions.

In 2023, it announced the launch of a high-payload firefighting programme by unveiling a fully functional prototype. The Firefighting unit is an autonomous, all-electric eVTOL that resembles AutoFlight's Prosperity passenger aircraft without windows and is a variant of the CarryAll cargo eVTOL.

The Firefighting model has a maximum take-off weight of two metric tonnes and a maximum payload weight of 400kg (882lb) over a distance up to 250km (155 miles) at speeds in excess of 200km/h (124mph).

It can carry four high-performance, fire-extinguishing canisters, each weighing 100kg (220lb), with each canister having capacity to extinguish fires covering up to 200m2. It has 13 propellers and electric motors, with ten VTOL-only propellers and three pusher propellers on the aircraft.

In December 2024, the CAAC granted a production certificate (PC) for AutoFlight's CarryAll unmanned cargo aircraft, which

▼ China is making a move into aerial firefighting using eVTOL unmanned aircraft. AutoFlight

▶ The AutoFlight CarryAll firefighting eVTOL can cover 155 miles at speeds in excess of 124mph. AutoFlight

was the world's first production licence for a two-ton eVTOL aircraft. Earlier in 2024, AutoFlight also received its type certificate and type design approval.

In partnership with local authorities, AutoFlight is building a new facility in the Central China city of Wuhan that will serve as

an assembly base and exhibition centre. Its operations will include handling aircraft final assembly, flight testing, sales, service, delivery and product promotion.

The partnership with Hanyang District will open the door for demonstration projects showcasing innovative applications in aerial firefighting, emergency response operations, air logistics and other relevant fields. AutoFlight said it will accelerate production scale-up and the commercial deployment of its large eVTOL aircraft.

The new facility was announced following the sale of 12 eVTOLs that will launch new air services in Wuhan. The order is for a mix of CarryAll autonomous aircraft and the five-seat Prosperity passenger-carrying model that will be used for applications including emergency

response missions, cargo carrying and for sightseeing flights along the Yangtze River.

AutoFlight is establishing a similar facility in East China where the city of Hefei has purchased multiple eVTOLs, including cargo models, emergency firefighting types and five-seat passenger aircraft. The city is partnering with AutoFlight to develop its 'low-altitude economy', including advanced air mobility services in the region.

With a population of more than ten million, Hefei is China's 18th largest city and has established itself as a leading low-altitude pilot city through supportive policies and innovative air traffic management systems. With its positive approach and enthusiasm for low-altitude opportunities, Hefei has become a model for urban centres across China.

▲ EHang is developing the firefighting aircraft in collaboration with local governments across China.
AutoFlight

◀ The AutoFlight Firefighting unit is based on the CarryAll cargo aircraft, a variant of the Prosperity passenger eVTOL.
AutoFlight

Rebuilding
Communities

Natural disasters and emergency situations progress through stages where aircraft play a vital role from the initial response to the aftermath; evacuating people, assessing damage and restoring power and communications infrastructures.

Emergencies usually demand an immediate response to contain and assess the incident, such as preventing a wildfire from getting out of control, offenders escaping the scene or transporting critically injured patients to hospital.

Once first responders have done their work it often turns to support agencies to move in and restore critical infrastructure, evacuate large numbers of displaced people, provide medical services or food and humanitarian aid. This is particularly the case when natural disasters such as earthquakes, floods, wildfires or hurricanes decimate populations and leave a trail of destruction in their wake.

Depending on the size of these events, governments typically call in the military for large-scale evacuations with their heavy aircraft, like Lockheed C-130 Hercules transports, that can deliver aid and specialist personnel on the way in and evacuate displaced people on the way out.

Helicopters also play a vital role and can often be seen plucking people off roofs in floods, dropping aid to those cut off from help and evacuating the injured from the scene. Helicopters shine in disaster missions that range from surveying damage, search and rescue, delivering supplies, medical evacuations, ferrying medical specialists to cut off areas and rebuilding infrastructure.

Restoring power and communications is a high priority and this is where aircraft have made significant contributions by allowing crews to inspect infrastructure and enable technicians to access damage where it is impossible to reach the area by land. This is also an area where drone technology coupled with real-time imaging and artificial intelligence (AI) can give controllers a clear picture of what needs to be done to restore vital services.

Samaritan's Purse

For more than 50 years, the nondenominational Christian organisation, Samaritan's Purse, has provided aid, materials and services to people displaced by natural disasters or impacted by disease, famine and war. It responds to emergency situations worldwide through its fleet of 24 aircraft, including the only active US-certified Douglas DC-8 jetliner.

Samaritan's Purse has a varied fleet that includes Boeing 757 and 767, Douglas DC-8 and DC-3 Twin Otter, Beech King Air, Cessna SkyHawk, SkyCourier and Grand Caravan, Kodiak and Piper PA-18 fixed-wing aircraft and Bell 407 and 412 helicopters.

The DC-8 is equipped to carry both cargo and passengers and is used to transport supplies and disaster assistance response teams where needed. It has a range of 7,000nm with 32 passengers and capacity for up to ten air-freight pallets with a combined weight of 74,000lb.

Also in the fleet is a de Havilland DHC-3 Twin Otter turboprop that was acquired in 2001. The 75-year-old aircraft was built for World War

▼ Samaritan's Purse has the only active US-certified Douglas DC-8. Samaritan's Purse

Two and is used as a workhorse for projects in Africa, including in the remotest parts of South Sudan. It can carry five tons of cargo or up to 32 passengers and is rugged enough to operate on unpaved runways.

The Douglas DC-8-72CF was the first civilian jet made by the company and it rolled off the assembly line on December 24, 1968. Samaritan's Purse rescued it from being scrapped for parts when it purchased the aircraft from an Australian cargo carrier in 2015 and completely refurbished it to meet FAA standards.

Just one day after it was cleared by the FAA, the DC-8 entered service with Samaritan's Purse in April 2016, airlifting an emergency field hospital, doctors, nurses and disaster response specialists to Ecuador after a 7.8-magnitude earthquake.

In March 2025, Myanmar and Thailand were devastated by a 7.7-magnitude earthquake that was followed just 12 minutes later by a 6.4-magnitude aftershock. More than 3,400 people lost their lives and countless more were injured. Samaritan's Purse immediately deployed the DC-8 carrying an emergency field hospital and 28 disaster response specialists, including doctors and nurses, to the ravaged area.

The emergency hospital provides 84 beds for surgical care and will also be equipped with an emergency room, laboratory, pharmacy and critical care unit. The organisation is also working to provide clean water, emergency shelter material, solar lights, hygiene kits and other relief supplies.

Samaritan's Purse used a Boeing 747 cargo aeroplane to carry more than 104 tons of critical supplies, including six water filtration systems from the US to Myanmar. The organisation has a long history in Myanmar where it responded to Cyclone Nargis in 2008 and maintained an office there between 2017 and 2022.

Since it was first deployed, the Douglas DC-8 has transported more

▲ The Samaritan's Purse fleet includes a DC-8 and Boeing 757. Samaritan's Purse

◀ Bell 412s and 407s delivered Samaritan's Purse aid after Hurricane Dorian. Samaritan's Purse

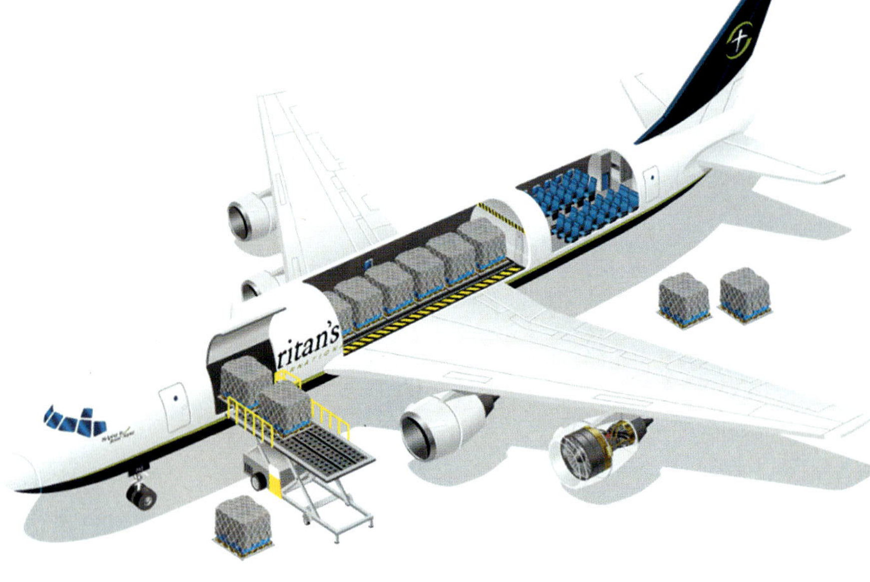

than 8.7 million pounds of cargo on over 200 missions worldwide, including to disasters in Haiti, Alaska, Mexico, Jamaica, Togo, Colombia, Tanzania, Ethiopia, Italy and Israel.

Aerial construction

When powerlines, pipelines and communications infrastructures are damaged during disasters the impact can spread well beyond the local area, affecting much larger populations and commercial activities in surrounding cities. Restoring those critical services is a high priority for local authorities and aircraft are increasingly playing a larger role in those missions.

The first step in restoring power is inspecting the powerlines and towers that are often traversing sensitive environments in difficult to access or remote locations, such as forests, mountains and swamps. This task was once the domain of workers with multiple teams driving the length of the line doing visual inspections from the ground or scaling towers to assess the transmission equipment.

With their ability to quickly access these environments, helicopters are now the vehicle of choice for emergency and routine infrastructure inspections with on-board crews able to safely inspect miles of lines in a single sweep. As the world turns to more renewable energy using offshore turbines, helicopters are also being deployed to inspect and repair wind farms located at sea or on land.

Single engine aircraft like the Airbus H125 are proving popular for powerline inspection while in the offshore and wind farm sector heavier aircraft such as the Airbus H135 and H145 are more prevalent, with repair work undertaken while the aircraft is in hover.

Depending on the mission, the aircraft are fitted with an array of high-technology cameras, including infrared ones that can detect hotspots and other thermal anomalies on transformers, powerlines and insulators. Ultraviolet cameras are used to find electricity leaks from equipment and lines that produce a corona discharge, which can lead to multiple performance and failure issues.

When a broader picture is required, operators can utilise light detection and ranging (LiDAR) technology on their aircraft to create detailed 3D models of powerline corridors. The LiDAR-generated images can assist crews and controllers to detect structural damage, sagging lines and other irregularities that may be impacting the security of supply.

Where infrastructure has been destroyed, helicopters can enable rebuilding from the air far more quickly than by ground crews and heavy construction equipment. The towers or other infrastructure can be assembled at a nearby staging ground and then flown into their final location to be lowered by the aircraft and positioned by the ground crews.

This is the way powerlines are being built in South American rainforests and other environmentally sensitive areas to minimise forest degradation. Helicopters like the Erickson S-64 Air Crane can fly the completed infrastructure and materials to the site and hang the wires, leaving the surrounding environment virtually untouched

mast mounted at a slight angle to each other.

This system has two primary advantages over conventional helicopters in that it brings increased efficiency and produces a natural tendency to hover. This generates more stability and makes the K-MAX more responsive to pilot controls, making it very suitable for placing suspended loads or hovering above ground crews, such as in forestry operations.

The K-MAX, also known as the Aerial Truck, was certified by the FAA in 1994 and in 2010 it successfully demonstrated unmanned helicopter cargo resupply to the US Marine Corps. The K-MAX operated as a pilotless aircraft in the Afghanistan conflict and between December 2019 and March 2020 it delivered more than 450 tons of cargo to combat areas.

The aircraft is powered by a Honeywell T531 gas turbine generating a top speed of 100kts and with three hours endurance and fuel consumption of 85g per hour, Kaman claims it has the most efficient fuel-to-lift ratio in its class. The K-MAX has an external load capacity of 6,000lb, a maximum take-off weight of 7,000lb and with no tail rotor or hydraulics requires less than two maintenance man-hours per flight hour.

The aircraft has been produced for both military and civilian operators and while the K-MAX is highly suited to heavy-lift missions, it has been adapted with specialised

◀ **Samaritan's Purse uses a fleet of 24 aircraft on global relief missions.** Samaritan's Purse

◀ **Helicopters play a vital role during flooding emergencies.** Airbus

▼◀ **Inspecting lines for damage and energy leakages from an AS350.** Airbus

▼ **Restoring and inspecting powerlines is quicker from the air.** Airbus

and without cutting long scars across the landscape.

Kaman's Aerial Truck

In 1945, Charles Kaman founded Kaman Corporation and just two years later his first rotary aircraft, the K-125 operated its inaugural flight. By 1954, Kaman had produced the first twin turbine-powered helicopter and also pioneered pilotless flights with the HTK-1 in 1957.

What makes Kamen aircraft instantly recognisable are the intermeshing twin-rotor design and the absence of a tail rotor, placing the aircraft in the synchropter category. Synchropters have a set of two main rotors turning in opposite directions with each rotor

▲ Erickson Air Cranes are well suited to alpine construction. Erickson

is ideal for loads too heavy for most helicopters and Rotex uses it on assembly work for powerlines, ski-lifts and moving heavy machinery.

From bases in Switzerland and Liechtenstein, Rotex teams regularly operate across France, Italy, Germany and Switzerland, travelling with ground crews and support vehicles. The K-MAX aircraft are supported with a heavy-duty JCB Helitrac, a fuel truck and a support vehicle carrying safety gear, cables, climbing and cutting equipment.

The K-MAX generates very little downwash and is quieter than most helicopters so it makes an ideal platform for working with climbers, tree cutters and flight assistants in close proximity.

A significant feature of the K-MAX is that it can lift up to 6,000lb and with an empty weight of 5,145lb it is one of the few helicopters with a

configurations for aerial firefighting and casualty evacuation.

Cleaning up debris

Wildfires and natural disasters leave a trail of destruction, blocking roads and preventing access to affected communities, particularly in forested areas. Specialist organisations employ helicopters to remove debris, such as fallen or dangerous trees, in areas where access by ground-based, heavy-lift equipment is impossible.

Founded in 1997, Swiss company Rotex Helicopter specialises in forestry and heavy-lift missions using Kaman K-Max aircraft while also carrying out firefighting and humanitarian missions in times of need. The K-MAX

▶ Kaman K-MAX is an intermeshing synchropter with no tail rotor. Kaman

▼ Swiss-based Rotex specialises in aerial construction using K-MAXs. Rotex

heavier payload than empty mass. Using an electric double hook allows for several loads to be carried on the same hook so each trip utilises the full payload capacity.

In challenging environments, Rotex uses a 'cut from the feet' forestry approach by attaching a line to a tree and hovering while the cutter removes the tree at the base or climbs to take off a section higher up. The pilot then lifts off with the tree underneath and carries it to a staging post where vehicle access is available.

In urban situations, this makes for a quick and clean method that requires no road access or heavy machinery on site and a task that would have taken a day can be completed in under an hour. In remote areas where access to communities is vital when disaster strikes, using aircraft such as the K-Max can open transport links to quickly move aid and specialists where needed.